Kimber Hoffman

W9-BQS-558

A MATTER OF CONSCIENCE

Court-martialed for his faith

A MATTER OF CONSCIENCE

Court-martialed for his faith

The gripping story of Harold Pervis and five
other sailors who defied wartime orders
and changed Naval history.

P. Harold Pervis, Sr.
with Norma Jean Lutz

REVIEW AND HERALD® PUBLISHING ASSOCIATION
HAGERSTOWN, MD 21740

Copyright © 1998 by
Review and Herald® Publishing Association
International copyright secured

The author assumes full responsibility for the accuracy of all facts
and quotations as cited in this book.

This book was
Edited by Penny Estes Wheeler
Designed by Bill Kirstein
Cover design by Bill Tymeson
Cover photo: Joel D. Springer
Typeset: 11.5/13 Weiss

PRINTED IN U.S.A.

02 01 00 99 98   5 4 3 2 1

R&H Cataloging Service
Pervis, Paul Harold, 1919-
    A matter of conscience: court-martialed
for his faith, by P. Harold Pervis, Sr., with Norma Jean
Lutz.

    1. Pervis, Paul Harold, 1919-   2. World War 1939-1945—
Conscientious objectors.   3. Conscientious objectors.
I. Lutz, Norma Jean, 1943-

                355.224

ISBN 0-8280-1087-0

DEDICATION

To my loving wife, Gracie, who also endured severe physical, financial, and emotional hardships during this time. For her prayers, extensive letter-writing efforts in securing our release, and continued love and support, I am eternally grateful.

To all those persons mentioned in this book who supported us with their prayers, visits, letters, and influence, I remain extremely grateful.

To all those many hundreds of people throughout the nation who through their letters and prayers gave us support, I am equally grateful.

To my fellow servicemen and women, may you find comfort in the fact that through everything, God is with us.

CHAPTER ONE

I watched as the ship's giant propellers churned the waters of the Atlantic, sending our troop carrier, U.S.S. *Antaeus*, farther out from the navy yard in Norfolk, Virginia. The tugs had broken away and were now tiny dots scurrying back to the safety of the harbor, while our big ship steamed out to the dangerous seas.

In the distance our destroyer escort maneuvered along like a mother whale protecting her young. While that presence should have given comfort, it only added to the element of tension, since I knew German submarines had often been detected in the Caribbean.

The *Antaeus* itself was equipped with long, gray antiaircraft guns and large spreads of antisubmarine depth charges. While we were still docked, I'd watched as the gunner mates made ready all the guns aboard our ship. The artillery was a vivid reminder that this was no holiday cruise. As part of the United States' effort against the German U-boat attacks on Atlantic shipping, the Navy maintained a strategic antisubmarine force on the island of Trinidad, off the north coast of Venezuela. The Navy hospital at Trinidad was my assigned destination.

Although I had grown up as a boy by the Manatee River in Florida, and although I'd been a sailor now for several months, this was my first experience on board a seagoing vessel. I was assigned to the third deck below, which was like being in a steel cave with hatches designed to close at various intervals in case of flooding in the compartments. The very word "flooding" made my stomach roll.

My first choice of military service would have been the Army. As a Seventh-day Adventist, it was important to me that the military understand my observance of Saturday—the Sabbath—as my day of worship. However, since it was so late in the war—1943—when I was inducted, there wasn't much choice involved.

After I passed the Army physical, I was informed that their quota was filled, and given a choice of the Navy or Marines. I'd heard the Navy was more lenient with those of the Adventist faith, so I chose the Navy.

Thankfully, a number of my Adventist buddies were with me on this trip. A draft of 10 Seventh-day Adventist hospital corpsmen were destined to report to the same hospital. Together, we spent a great deal of time out on the deck to get away from the cigarette smoke and card games.

Russell Pitrone, a short Italian boy, and I had known each other since training school. He was barely 19, with dark eyes and a mop of dark curly hair, an impish smile, and a marvelous gift of gab. We talked for hours about the families we'd left behind. My beautiful wife, Gracie, and my son, Paul junior, were constantly on my mind. I was greatly concerned as to how they would fare without me there to look after them.

Harry Buckley, at age 33, was the "papa" of our group. Vesterlide Alden was next in line at age 27. These two were family men, having left behind wives and children, as I had. I was next oldest at 25, and the others were young, single guys like Pitrone.

The *Antaeus*, along with the accompanying destroyer, set

a zigzag pattern through the Atlantic with Bermuda as its first stop. We stood on deck and admired its rocky shoreline and trim white houses. After only a few hours we were under way once again, and one day followed another in quiet monotony. Since I and the other corpsmen were being transported, there was no work to keep our hands and minds occupied. Boredom was our constant companion.

One night we were jolted awake by loud explosions reverberating throughout the ship. Fear leaped up inside me, but almost instantly a verse came to my mind: "The angel of the Lord encampeth round about them that fear him, and delivereth them" (Psalm 34:7). In the weeks to come, that verse often was a source of comfort to me.

The next day we were told that a German submarine had been sighted and the explosions we felt were depth charges being thrown from both our ship and the destroyer.

The scenery around the Caribbean Islands was beautiful—the vivid aqua and green-blue waters and small islands covered in thick vegetation. We put in overnight at San Juan, Puerto Rico, but no shore leave was granted.

Finally, after many days at sea, the U.S.S. *Antaeus* moved through the Dragon's Mouth Strait, as it is known, separating the tip of Venezuela from the Chacachacare Islands of Trinidad. When Christopher Columbus first saw this island, he was stirred by three prominent mountain peaks and quickly named it *La Trinidad* for the Holy Trinity. I was entranced by the intense violet-blue of the waters, and the jagged island mountains rising sharply out of the sea. I longed to explore this fascinating place, but never had an opportunity to do so.

The coxswain's shrill whistle sounded over the loudspeakers as the ship steered carefully through the antisubmarine nets guarding the harbor. Next we heard the call for all men reporting for duty at the U.S. Naval Operating Base, Port of Spain, Trinidad, to prepare to debark.

I struggled down the steep gangplank, top-heavy with my load of gear. All my earthly possessions were on my back and slung over my shoulder. The coxswain stood at the foot of the gangplank with a clipboard and pencil in hand. "Sound off as you come by," he ordered.

Over the racket and commotion of cargo being unloaded, I shouted my name: "Pervis, Paul H." Two dozen of us reported for this new detail. Unfortunately, the large influx of sailors would overload the hospital personnel causing a serious problem for me and my friends later on.

Solid land under my feet felt wonderful, but it took a while to lose the sensation of rocking on the high seas. The balmy air caressing my face reminded me of Florida. After a short wait we saw an olive drab truck lumbering toward us. Throwing our gear in the back, we crawled in after it.

We were taken to the chow hall, where we ate a welcome supper. What a luxury to once again eat sitting down. On board ship we ate standing at a chest-high table board—not exactly the latest thing in comfort. Also, standing in the ship's chow line meant being constantly exposed to the heavy aromas from nearby garbage. I had not eaten well during the entire trip, and was ravenously hungry.

Well fed, we returned to the dock to wait for the truck that would take us to our destination. Evening was closing in and the sky's lavender tint sky softened the green hue of the jungle. Already I had spotted a number of familiar palms and plants native to Florida. The bamboo were plentiful, and a sprawling mango tree reminded me of the one in the front yard of my boyhood home on Sneads Island. I felt right at home.

When a truck rolled up beside us, a Navy NCO jumped

out and called muster. We threw in our gear and loaded into the back. The truck pulled out of the staging area, moved out of the main gate of the base, and chugged slowly along a winding road that led upward toward the hospital. Tucker Valley Naval Hospital was situated five miles inland through the thick tropical jungle.

At the hospital, in typical Navy fashion, we were unloaded and then quickly loaded again when the driver discovered we should have been taken directly to our quarters. One more time we hefted our gear into the back of the truck. The barracks were located up the hill from the hospital. In the dim twilight, we could see that they were long buildings situated on high stilts.

The NCO once again ordered us out, and the noise of scuffling men and thudding seabags filled the night air. The moment we were unloaded, the truck sped away. Shouldering our bags, we made our way up the steps.

The quarters were partitioned into cubicles, each with double-deck bunks, steel lockers, desks, and lamps. Pure Navy luxury at its finest. We could hardly believe our good fortune. Rather than having regular windows, the barracks were fitted with wire screens beneath deep, eight-foot eaves. The wide eaves provided protection from the tropical rains, and yet allowed constant ventilation.

After so many days at sea our first priority was to hurry to the shower. Fresh water felt far better than washing with seawater on board ship. When we returned from our showers I was surprised to hear a voice call out my name. "Pervis! Welcome to Tucker Valley."

"Hey, Riggs," I called back. "Good to see you again."

James Riggs had been stationed with me in San Diego, but he'd been shipped directly from there to the hospital in

Trinidad. His wife, Mildred, traveled with Gracie and me as we drove across country from San Diego to Virginia. It was great to see him once again. Riggs was working in the hospital lab and told us how much he enjoyed his duty there.

The first thing we wanted to know from this fellow Adventist was the climate toward those of our faith.

"The SDAs are known and appreciated at Tucker Valley," he explained. "I don't think you'll have any problems here. I did hear that the departing crew hasn't yet shipped out, so you may have other assignments for a while."

I found myself breathing a little easier with this bit of good news. With each new station, each of us harbored our own bit of concern that we might be ordered to break our observance of the Bible Sabbath.

"By the way," Riggs added, "we hold Sabbath school in the hospital bomb shelter every Friday evening at 2000 [8:00]. Hope to see you there."

I fell asleep that night to the sweet orchestration of various bird calls from deep in the thick of the jungle. I felt a peace deep inside, and was glad to be on this tour of duty.

The next morning, Friday, we were ordered to report to the hospital administration building at 0800. This sprawling complex, which had literally been carved out of the dense, ever-growing jungle, stood ready to receive the overflow of wounded sailors coming in from Europe.

Dressed in our Navy whites, we stood outside the office of Commander Vaughn, the executive officer. When told he could see us, we filed into his large office and stood at attention before his wide mahogany desk. Commander Vaughn was a rotund gentleman with a ruddy complexion. After ordering us "at ease," he proceeded to brief us on the installation and the operation details.

We were told the policies and procedures as they pertained to the hospital corpsmen, followed by various warnings about leave conduct in the nearby city of Port of Spain. We also learned that the commander hailed from my home state of Florida. "Now," he said, "I'd like to hear what kinds of hospital experience you've had, what types of specialized training you've received outside of corps school, as well as the type of duty you prefer here at Tucker Valley. We'll do all we can to place you where your training can be utilized."

Pitrone said he'd been in the Merchant Marine service before enlisting in the Navy, and that he'd accumulated considerable medical experience aboard ship. Montgomery explained about his laboratory experience, and Boundey described his X-ray and surgical nursing work.

Before dismissing us, the executive officer had a serious last word. "You're here in my office on friendly terms at this moment," he began. His eyes narrowed. "If you're ever in here again, it'll be because you're in some kind of trouble."

Unfortunately, that situation presented itself less than 24 hours later!

From his office we were directed down the passageway to the office of the chief master at arms, where we were to receive our duty assignments. After only a brief wait, we were welcomed into Chief Howland's office. This tall, serious man outlined to us the types of jobs that would soon become available at the hospital. Then he concluded, "I regret that the men whom you will be replacing have not yet received their orders. You will, therefore, be given temporary duty assignment. They'll be ready for you tomorrow morning." And with that we were dismissed.

The rest of the day was ours to do with as we liked. After stowing our gear and completing laundry detail, we eagerly explored the area. I found myself constantly pointing out to my buddies all the palms I knew—and naming them. My family had grown palm trees for many years in Florida, and I knew many of the types we were now seeing.

Just before 2000 [8:00] that evening we made our way to the bomb shelter to attend Sabbath school. Worshiping on the seventh day of the week (as instructed in Exodus 20:8-11), we observed the Sabbath from sundown on Friday until sundown on Saturday.

Seventh-day Adventists keep the Sabbath holy as a service rendered to God through the consecration of the 24 hours of the seventh day of the week. Keeping the Sabbath is far more than sandwiching in an hour or two of worship on that day, but rather a means of wholly serving God. On the Sabbath, the day God has sanctified (Genesis 2:3), we seek to offer God the service of our total being.

While we are fully ready to reach out to help others during the Sabbath, we refrain from work, as such. This adherence is not a duty, or a rule to be obeyed, but a day to share God's blessings with others.

Before we reached the bomb shelter, we heard the strains of a familiar hymn being played on an old government-issue pump organ. The warmth of that hymn reached out and enveloped each of us with its comforting effect.

We discovered that the service consisted of singing, prayers, mission stories, and a Bible lesson study. Some of us newcomers were asked to participate; in fact, Buckley was elected the new superintendent. Sadly, however, he would never have the opportunity to assume that responsibility. The events of the next day—our first Sabbath in Trinidad—would not only change Buckley and all our group, but were destined to change the policies of the entire United States Navy.

CHAPTER TWO

I felt an air of anticipation following the worship service, and found it difficult to sleep. Worshiping with the others had given me strength and comfort. However, my longing to see Gracie and little Paul intensified, not only because of the quiet night hours, but also because it was Sabbath. To Adventists, Sabbath is traditionally a special time of "togetherness" for families. Earlier in the day I'd written a long letter to Gracie, describing the beauties of the island and explaining that I anticipated a good tour of duty at Tucker.

Sleep eventually took over, and the next thing I heard was the cracking of a wooden baton against a steel bed frame and the night watch shouting, "Out of those sacks, men! Hit the deck!"

It was 0600 (6:00), and the barracks sprang to life as men scurried to the showers and pulled on their uniforms. We newcomers often heard "Where are you from?" A sailor far from home clung to the hope he might meet someone from his home state—or better yet, from his hometown. As luck would have it, I discovered a fellow I'd known in my college days in Tennessee. It's difficult to explain what a warm feeling that gave me. Somehow it lessened my sensation of being "displaced."

Following an ample breakfast of scrambled eggs and fried

potatoes, we had time to browse about the grounds until time to report for duty. "I wonder what kind of duty we'll pull today?" I mused aloud.

Montgomery, who had a penchant for math and chemistry, said he hoped he'd be sent to the lab.

"I don't care what I get," Pitrone told us, an air of apprehension in his voice, "as long as it's something I can do on the Sabbath."

A few minutes before 0800 we sat down outside the office of Chief Master at Arms Howland. Buckley had become our unofficial spokesman. He approached the yeoman on duty and told him we were reporting as ordered.

As we waited small talk bounced around among our group almost as though we needed the noise to mask our uneasiness. Facing a new duty assignment on a Sabbath morning was always a little worrisome. A full half hour passed—typical in the armed forces—but especially unsettling to us as we waited and wondered.

Suddenly the office door opened and the chief emerged in a cloud of cigarette smoke, a sheaf of yellow papers in one hand, a smoldering cigarette in the other.

He looked at us intently, then said, "Please stand by, men," and reentered his office and closed the door.

"I wouldn't want to tangle with that guy," Alden said softly. "He doesn't seem like the friendliest person around."

"Wonder what's holding things up?" said Boundey, glancing at his watch once again. But no one answered. We were all lost in our own thoughts.

After another long wait, Chief Howland once again burst forth from his office, this time with a fresh cigarette. We jumped to our feet as he approached.

"Alden, Vesterlide S.," the chief called out, scanning the faces before him.

It took a minute for Alden to realize his name had actually been called. The chief repeated, "Alden, Vesterlide S.!"

"Here, sir. I mean, present, sir," he stammered. The repressed nervousness came bubbling to the surface.

"Better wake up, mate," the chief warned. Beginning with Alden, he called the roll going down the list alphabetically. When the roll was completed, he took a long draw from the cigarette before continuing. "Men, I regret to inform you that the hospital assignments that you are to fill are not yet available. Until those whom you are relieving receive their orders, you will be given temporary assignments with the grounds department." He stopped a moment to study the papers in his clipboard, then looked back at our little group standing before him. "You will ship immediately into your work dungarees and report to the master at arms in charge of grounds maintenance. That's all."

We all just stood there, stunned. I felt my heart thudding in my chest. Suddenly the lament of the biblical Job was painfully real to me. *"For the thing which I greatly feared is come upon me"* (Job 3:25). Now what were we to do?

This time it was Montgomery who regained his composure enough to speak. He stepped up behind the retreating chief. Hearing the footsteps, Chief Howland turned around coming face-to-face with Montgomery.

"Chief," Montgomery began, probably with more calm in his voice than he felt inside, "we're all Seventh-day Adventist Christians. We observe the seventh day of the week, Saturday, as the Sabbath of the Bible. Although the Bible forbids us to do nonessential types of work on the Sabbath, we are eager to attend the sick on God's holy day, just as Jesus did. But our consciences will not permit us to perform the type of work you have asked us to do on the Sabbath."

17

✮✮

The silence following Montgomery's words was deafening. A look of shock and disbelief registered on the ruddy face of Chief Howland. But the shock soon switched to intense anger. His dark eyes fairly burned.

To his credit, Montgomery did not wilt. Rather he added, "We would gladly make up our time if you allow us this Sabbath day off—"

The sentence was never finished. "You are not deaf! I did not stutter," the chief stormed at us. "Get changed into dungarees and report to the grounds master at arms *on the double!* That is all!"

He turned on his heel and marched into his office, slamming the door as an emphatic punctuation to his final order. The yeoman sitting at his desk shook his head. He looked at us, then looked at the closed door and looked back at us. I could fairly read his thoughts—that no one made this chief angry without paying a high cost.

We were too stunned to move. We searched one another's faces in hopes someone would have an idea what we should do next. Finally, giving a shrug, Boundey turned and moved toward the door. We followed in abject silence.

"What'll we do now?" I asked. I didn't really believe any one of us had a solid answer, but I felt we needed to talk this out.

Pitrone had faced this problem before, so he answered first. "I suggest we simply follow the chief's orders as far as we can short of sabotaging our consciences. We need to show that we are willing to obey as far as we possibly can."

Of course, none of us thought that would solve the problem, but it at least gave us the next step to take. Buckley agreed with Pitrone. "You're exactly right," he said, his wide square jaw set in determination. "It's our duty to follow orders as far as we can."

One of the others didn't see it that way. "We'll have to stop somewhere," he countered. "It might as well be now. I vote for stopping right now and getting it over with. Why drag it out?"

After a considerable amount of discussion, the majority agreed with Pitrone. We would follow the chief's bidding as far as we could with a clear conscience.

When we arrived at the barracks two or three of the men threw a few necessary toilet articles into their ditty bags and laid them on their bunks—just in case. I chose to follow suit. None of us knew what might happen next.

Our clothes changed, we walked across the compound. The tin shack we were looking for was tucked back in a corner of the clearing. We were met at the door by outside Master at Arms Martin. Buckley, resuming his position as our spokesman, stepped forward.

"Sir," he said, unable to disguise the note of urgency in his voice, "we are Seventh-day Adventist Christians. Today, Saturday, is the Sabbath, the day that we believe the Bible instructs us to keep holy."

Not detecting any anger from Martin, Buckley continued. "We're more than willing to perform acts of humanitarian benefits just as Jesus did on the Sabbath. But our consciences will not allow us to perform types of labor that do not directly relate to relieving human suffering on God's holy day."

Perhaps it was shock and surprise that kept the outside master at arms from replying, but Buckley kept talking as fast as he possibly could. "We would appreciate it very much, sir, if you might postpone our duties until after sundown this evening."

Feeling a burst of confidence from Buckley's presentation, I stepped up to his side and added, "Sir, we'll gladly work tomorrow, or tonight, or anytime, to make up our work duties."

The MA looked at each of us as if he were waiting for someone to tell him this was a joke. After a moment, he said, "Is the
whole lot of you telling me you refuse to work this detail?"

"Yes, sir," I answered.

The MA lifted his cap and situated it once again on his
head. "You're all refusing to do *any* work today on the
grounds—is that what you're telling me?"

"We'll be more than willing to do humanitarian work
today," Boundey told him, "or to do our grounds work after
sundown this evening. But we cannot do maintenance work
on the Sabbath, sir. Our consciences simply will not allow it."

Once again that deafening silence filled the air. It was
clear that an impasse was at hand.

The MA shook his head. "Let's go see the chief then."

Stepping inside the shed, he grabbed his clipboard and
then headed out across the grounds of the compound with the
10 of us in a line behind him. As we walked along, the other
sailors on grounds detail stopped their work of chopping and
hacking at the dense jungle to watch our little parade.

Shortly, we arrived back where we started, in front of the
door of Chief Howland's office. The door opened and the
chief stepped out almost as if he were expecting us. "So
what's the matter with you men?" he demanded as we all
snapped to attention. Without waiting for any one of us to
reply, he turned to the MA. "Tell me what happened."

"They refuse to work," came the answer. "Something
about their Sabbath. They just won't work."

The chief was undoubtedly a man who was deeply
trained in the ways of the military. He'd been taught to obey
at all costs, and expected nothing less from his subordinates.
This was an unthinkable reproach to him.

"This is the United States Navy," Howland's voice boomed in our ears. "I'm ordering you men to go and do as you have been ordered to do—*now*—or there will be trouble." His face flushed red as he said each measured word. "I can be a good man when I'm obeyed, but I can be mean when I am not obeyed."

Chief Howland then motioned for MA Martin to come into his office. The two disappeared behind the door as we stood in a line outside waiting. Personnel continually walked up and down the busy hallway, casting a nervous eye in our direction. Being set on public display was not a comfortable experience.

At last Howland and Martin emerged and strode down the hall to the office of Executive Officer Vaughn. I glanced at the others, but all appeared calm despite the situation.

After a moment the exec's office door opened once more, and the MA came toward us. "The exec wants to see you fellows, pronto."

We walked uneasily into the office of Executive Officer Commander Vaughn and snapped to attention. For an endless moment the exec stared into the face of each of the 10 of us. His voice was tense and tight as he asked, "What's the matter here?"

Buckley, his voice now quavering a bit, clearly explained our position and once again asked that we have the Sabbath off or be given humanitarian work to do.

By now the exec's voice was trembling as well, but certainly not from fear. His face was rigid and his neck muscles quivered like tightly wound fiddle strings. "To _____ with your religion! This is the United States Navy!" He slammed the desk with his powerful fist. "We are a nation at war, and this hospital runs on a seven-day workweek."

Then for a split second he seemed to grab a semblance of self-control. "Now listen to me. I'm as good a Christian as any of you, but I have to work on Sunday and I don't like it any more than you do." His voice came slower now and more even. "You men go to work *now*. I'll have no more of this nonsense. If you come to this office again, I'll take you to the captain. Dis-*missed!*"

Back in the hallway, the chief restated his position. "It's just as important to keep the outside of this compound well kept and manicured as it is to give bedside care inside," he told us.

But again, we had to tell him respectfully we were unable to do so.

"Picking up a few little papers on your Sabbath won't hurt anyone's religion," he quipped, attempting now to wear us down. He searched our faces for signs that one of us might be changing his mind or experiencing a crumbling of will. But he saw nothing. We were, to a man, united in devotion to our belief.

Now his face softened somewhat, and his voice became almost gentle. "Men, just go out and report for duty, but then only walk around and pretend to be busy while you're not really working."

To the chief's dismay, none of us answered this new twist on his reasoning. Time stretched out slowly as he waited. Suddenly, in exasperation, he and the grounds MA pushed through our group and proceeded back toward the office of the executive officer. Presently, he and the exec emerged and strode on down the hall to the office labeled Commanding Officer.

I felt my spirits lift somewhat, since I felt that surely Captain Tabor would understand our position and would act accordingly.

Before being led into the captain's office, I pulled from my pocket a neatly folded and well-worn piece of paper. This copy of Navy Personnel Circular Letter No. 115-43 stated that men wishing to observe a day other than Sunday were to be given consideration—that is, providing their commanding officer deemed it appropriate. The wording was somewhat ambiguous, but it was all we had to support our position.

Captain Tabor, an older man with graying temples, was dressed in an impeccable white uniform with four gold braids on the shoulder boards. Warm, friendly sunshine streamed in through the windows and shone off the gold braids. Dressed in our faded dungarees, we stood at attention before his desk. The officer surveyed us with interest. Although frightened, we each felt a measure of peace in our choice to hold firm to what we believed.

Captain Tabor asked what the problem was, and spokesman Buckley once again presented our beliefs and position as best he could. As he spoke, Chief Howland, grounds Master at Arms Martin, and other officers stood about the room listening as well.

When Buckley had finished speaking, I unfolded Circular No. 115-43 and handed it to Captain Tabor, but he calmly brushed it aside.

"Men, this is the Navy of the United States of America. In this Navy you are expected to obey the commands of your superior officers." The captain paused and cleared his throat. "This morning you reported to the outside master at arms for duty, but then refused to obey his command to work."

I felt perspiration break out on my forehead as he looked squarely at each one of us and slowly continued. "Now men, I am going to repeat the command that was given previ-

23

ously. Go to work, as you have been instructed. This is a warning. The next time you come before me, I will take severe action. *Excused!"*

I felt shaken to the core as we walked out of the captain's office. He was our last hope of receiving an understanding audience. The deadlock had intensified. There was no turning back.

CHAPTER THREE

Strangely enough, the chief now let down his guard and displayed a twinge of regret. He tried once again to talk us into reconsidering our decision and just "get on out there and get to work."

The chief knew, and we knew, that the matter was now totally out of his hands. Since it had come to the attention of the captain, and since the captain had echoed their orders, there was nothing at all the exec or the chief could do. There was no alternative but to return the 10 of us to the exec's office.

The exec heaved a sigh. "I'll have to take you to the captain again," he said flatly.

A knot of nervousness twisted deep in my midsection as we once again faced the captain.

Captain Tabor took the roster sheet from the chief. "I'm going to ask each one of you men, individually, whether you will, here and now, obey the lawful order of your superior officer and go to work"

A legal officer stood to the left of his desk. It was an ominous sign.

"Alden, Vesterlide S."

"Here, sir."

"Do you here and now refuse to obey the lawful order of your superior officers to go to work as you have been instructed?"

"Sir, I must refuse because—"

He was cut short. "You are to answer the question 'Yes,' or 'No.'"

Calmly Alden gave his reply. "Yes, sir."

In the quiet that followed, I heard the scratching of the legal officer's pen as he scribbled notes on his tablet.

Boundey was questioned next. He echoed Alden. One by one we were required to answer the captain's question. When all 10 of our names were read, when all 10 had answered, and our answers were recorded, the captain pronounced our sentence: "I hereby sentence you men to five days in the Marine brig at the Naval Operating Base. There you will have time to think things over."

This formal procedure was known as Captain's Mast. We had just been given a deck court-martial by this captain. In that moment I was no longer just a sailor in the Navy. Instead, I was now a prisoner of the Navy.

We had disobeyed a direct order in the matter of freedom of religion and worship, one of the basic freedoms for which we were at war to preserve. An ironic twist.

At the sharp command of a shore patrol guard who had been called in for just this purpose, we were marched out of Captain Tabor's office. The clank and jangle of handcuffs hanging from the belts of the guards was unsettling to our ears.

We were marched to the mess hall, where we were fed our noon meal. Of course, our churning stomachs allowed us to eat only a little. I kept wondering what had gone wrong. It was all so confusing. This would be our last meal at the Tucker Valley Naval Hospital, though we didn't know so at the time.

From the mess hall we were marched back to the barracks to gather all our personal items—including our

Bibles—which we crammed quickly into the ditty bags. Montgomery grabbed his expensive harmonica, which he could play quite well.

With our bags slung over our shoulders, we were marched to the dispensary for preconfinement physicals. Word about our incident must have swept through the compound, because heads peeked from every corner and out the windows. Now and then we even heard a soft voice murmur, "Good luck," or "Stick with it, fellows." As I thought of the incident later, their words brought me comfort, but at the moment I was too numb to think.

The green-and-tan camouflaged truck came to a stop in the gravel of the hospital staging area. Jumping down from the truck, hitting the gravel with a thud, were two broad-shouldered Navy guards. In their arms they carefully cradled their shotguns. The Navy guards shouted out our names, and we shouted "Here," as one by one we jumped into the idling truck and sat down on the slatted board seats.

By the time we were all loaded, the daily rain of Trinidad had begun, splatting noisily on the canvas truck canopy. One Navy guard took his place at the front of the truck, the other at the rear. They struggled to keep their balance as the truck lurched forward to the sound of grinding gears.

We left the hospital grounds and slowly rumbled up the narrow mountain road. As the canvas flapped open and closed I could see the plantations of banana and sugarcane along the way, interspersed with the raw, thick jungle growth.

Five days, I reasoned to myself. Five days wasn't very long. I could handle five days in the clink. Once this glitch was taken care of, everything would be back to normal. The thought of returning to duty on this lush tropical island would help me get through the next few days.

We arrived at the main gate of the base itself where the truck paused momentarily, then surged onward through the network of barracks and various buildings. Suddenly it slowed and stopped. The rumbling engine was silent. We heard the driver's boots hit the gravel, then clump noisily up the creaky wooden stairs. The wooden door of the brig opened and slammed shut again.

At that, the two guards relaxed their weapons. My nine buddies and I sat in silence, occasionally glancing at one another's strained faces—trying not to look at the stoic faces of the guards. One guard fished in his pocket for a cigarette and lit up in the close quarters of the truck. Soon the area was filled with thick, gray smoke. Time seemed to stand still. Suddenly the pattering rain let up and the sun broke out, turning the canvas-covered truck into a steamy sauna. Sweat trickled down my face, but I didn't dare move to wipe it away. The slatted seat became more and more uncomfortable. At length, we began to fidget and squirm.

When the brig door opened again, we heard several pairs of boots clomp down the steps, then surround the truck. Silence again. Once again the brig door opened and boots came down the steps and stopped at the rear of the truck. From there a voice boomed out, "OK, prisoners, *out!* Form a line facing me. Let's *go,* prisoners!"

Now we saw the gun-toting guards surrounding the truck, and a tall Marine master sergeant waiting for us to line up pronto. This tall, blond sergeant named Kurzak was the epitome of a Marine with square shoulders, bulging muscles, and a perpetual scowl. He was obviously the warden, for his belt supported a gun and holster, a billy club, and a key ring full of jangling keys. I felt as though his eyes could burn holes through me. Not a movement escaped his careful, constant scrutiny.

Once the body count was completed, he waved the truck away and we were left in the hands of these new keepers.

We soon learned that Sergeant Kurzak shouted every word that came out of his mouth. "Prisoners!" he bellowed as he pointed, "line up in front of those steps—on the *double!*"

We ran forward and slid to a stop in front of the steps where he had directed. The guards ran alongside, keeping a watchful eye on this new little band of prisoners. Sergeant Kurzak then slowly mounted the steps and turned about to look at us. His bass voice called out once again. "Every man come up these steps as I call your name, on the *double*, then into the holding room ahead of you." He pointed toward the brig door.

"OK! Alden, Vesterlide S. Let's *go!*"

Alden sped up the stairs with his ditty bag flying behind him. He shouted his name at the top and ran through the door, which was opened by a corporal.

One by one we ran up the stairs as our names were called, until all 10 of us stood in the holding room. I felt sorry for Alden, since he was always the first to be called. Now he was called forward to the desk. As he did so, the sergeant's deep voice called out, *"Attention,* prisoner. This here's the brig, not a vacation resort! Look sharp, there."

Alden was asked his rating, serial number, and place of origin, and was given a list of brig regulations. He was then asked to hand over his valuables. The guard placed them in a cupboard there in the holding room for "safekeeping," as they called it. He was then told to put his ditty bag in a storage room that was near the head (toilet).

The storage room and the head were the only rooms in the entire brig with solid enclosed walls. The rest of the brig consisted of waist-high walls around the perimeter, but all the inside enclosures were created by steel bars, screen wire, or chain-link cyclone fencing. I could look down the expanse of the brig through the fencing to the very end, obstructed only by the neat rows of double bunks.

This arrangement looked more like cages than cells. It also gave the resident prisoners ample opportunity to watch our arrival. They were obviously pleased that their work detail had been halted for the afternoon until our group was cared for. At the far end from where we stood was a concrete vaultlike structure, the solitary confinement cells. We would learn more about those later.

When Alden came back to the desk the guard motioned him toward one of the enclosures. The guard unlocked the heavy padlock and lifted it from the hasp's loop, and the door was opened. Alden walked through and flopped down on the lower bunk.

I shuddered as the door slammed shut.

Next it was Boundey's turn. He, too, was relieved of his valuables and made to stow his ditty bag. Down the list, each name was called in order. I watched as Montgomery handed over his expensive harmonica. It was the last time he ever saw it.

When my name was called, I too gave over the few things I had in my pockets and stowed my bag. Suddenly I felt empty and vulnerable. I was placed in the enclosure with the others. The bunk above Alden's was empty, holding only a tightly rolled blue-and-white-striped, very lumpy, cotton mattress. Neatly folded beside the mattress was a gray-green woolen blanket marked with a faded Marine Corps emblem. The "springs" on the bed were a series of wooden slats nailed crosswise to the wooden frame of the bunk's support rails.

It was just after 12:00, but the day already seemed interminably long. I mused to myself the irony of the fact that while the Navy cared for the wounded and sick Marines, it was the Marines who guarded the Navy prisoners. An interesting trade-off.

Once all of our group had been placed in an enclosure, the other prisoners were called out for work detail. Suddenly it dawned on me that we might once again be asked to work on the Sabbath—now with the prison detail.

After the other prisoners had filed out we were issued regulation gear for the brig—dungaree pants and shirts. They were clean but faded and nearly threadbare. The back of each shirt and front of each pant leg sported a large white letter "P," which had been crudely painted on the cloth.

Like a crack of thunder, the voice of the warden broke the silence, calling us to attention. We were ordered to "hit the black line on the double." The black line, we soon learned, was a line in front of the warden's desk. We stepped lively from our unlocked cage to the warden's office.

As we stood stiffly at attention before his desk, we heard someone coming up the steps and into the brig. It was a wizened little man, a Trinidad national, carrying a worn leather satchel, which he set down on the warden's desk with a thud. His dull eyes and expressionless face told us he'd been there before.

We had no idea what was happening, but the old man slowly pulled an ancient pair of hand-operated hair clippers from the satchel.

"Now," crooned Marine Sergeant Kurzak in a singsong voice, "we're gonna make you prisoners look real purty." In less than 30 seconds all of Alden's hair was sheared from his head and scattered about the floor. In the usual alphabetical order each of us fell under the man's clippers.

The old clippers hadn't been oiled or sharpened in a good many days. But the sting from the hair-pulling clippers was the least part of our discomfort. Being stripped of our dignity struck a much deeper pain. Now with our shaved heads and dressed in faded prison garb, we were inducted as full-fledged prisoners of the U.S. Navy.

We were sent itching and scratching back to our cages. Without the talc and nice brushing of a normal barbershop, prickly hairs clung to our sweaty bodies. I'd barely sat down on my bunk when another order was shouted through the brig. "Alden, Boundey, and Buckley!" boomed the sergeant. "Let's go to work, prisoners. Hit the black line on the double."

Oh no, I thought. *Here we go again.*

"What's wrong with you prisoners? You hard of hearing or something? Let's *go*, prisoners!"

With barely a backward glance at the rest of us, the three men burst forth out of the cages, back down the walkway to the warden's office, and stood behind the now-infamous black line. Unfortunately, their line and posture didn't meet the expectation of the warden, so he spent several long minutes castigating them for the inability to stand at attention correctly. It seemed to be his delight to shout and yell at whatever and whomever, on a regular basis.

The warden took the roster clipboard from his desk and ordered his three new prisoners to sound off as they ran by his desk and out the door. "And I want to be able to hear you a mile away!"

I had no doubt that Alden, Boundey, and Buckley would refuse to work, no matter what was threatened. And I was right. Boundey later described what happened.

They ran past Kurzak's desk, sounding off by number, running out the door and down the stairs, almost into the arms of an armed guard. The shotgun he held was pointed directly at the three men. The "chaser," as he was called, ran alongside them as they marched along double time.

They were led to a camouflaged Quonset hut where the tools were stored. Here they stopped and were each given a large machete. Again, they were expected to hack away at the thick jungle growth around the base.

The tension mounted as they stood there for a moment. Presently, Buckley stepped forward and said, "Sir, we are Seventh-day Adventist hospital corpsmen. Today, Saturday, is the Sabbath of the Bible, and the Bible forbids us to do this kind of work on the Sabbath day."

The chaser stared at Buckley in disbelief, his face growing red. He shifted his stance to parade rest and raised the shotgun and clicked off the safety catch.

"You're telling me all you fellows are refusing to work?"

Obviously, he'd never been faced with such a sticky dilemma. His lips trembled and sweat broke out on his brow. His right forefinger moved slowly to the weapon's trigger. "You know I can use this if I have to," he said evenly as he moved the muzzle from one man to the next.

The prisoners knew full well he had every right to use the shotgun if he interpreted their action as mutiny. Especially in light of the fact that the U.S. was in a state of war.

For an endless moment, the chaser studied each of the three faces. At length, his decision was to take them back to Sergeant Kurzak and let him handle the matter. Each man released an inward sigh of relief as the chaser clicked the safety back on. The chaser trotted double time leading them from the Quonset hut back around the weaving pathways to the brig.

From inside the brig, we heard footsteps coming, and we

glanced at one another and nodded. We knew what had happened. It seemed strange that the rest of us had not been sent out. Could this have been another test?

We watched as the sergeant stood just inside the door waiting, his arms folded and a deep scowl on his brow. "What's the problem?" he demanded of the chaser as the group entered.

"They won't work."

"Won't work, eh?"

"No, sir."

"Do you fellows know the penalty for disobeying the order of a superior officer of the United States Marine Corps in time of war?" Of course, all 10 of us knew. "We'll just see about this. Put 'em back in," he shouted.

Sergeant Kurzak then addressed the rest of our group. "Do all of you refuse to work?"

In unison we answered, "Yes, sir."

At that point, we could hear the warden furiously dialing the phone on his desk. "Give me the commander of the Marine garrison!" he yelled into the phone. Then he was quiet. There were bits of conversation I couldn't make out. I struggled to make the taut muscles in my body relax. The time was now 1400. Just 2:00 p.m. This was the longest Sabbath I'd ever experienced in my life.

The next sounds we heard were boots stomping up the stairs. A short, graying Marine Corps major, named MacArthur, entered the brig. The warden stood, snapped to attention, and saluted. Major MacArthur acknowledged, and then the two of them buzzed in lowered voices. It was the first time since we arrived that the warden had spoken in a soft tone. As they conversed, the major kept glancing down the run at our strange little group.

Presently, the major pulled out the warden's chair and sat

down behind the desk. He asked that the prisoners be brought before him two at a time. Alden and Boundey, of course, were first.

The cage was opened, and Alden and Boundey double-timed it to the desk and snapped at attention.

"Now what's the trouble, sailor?" Major MacArthur asked.

As before, Alden explained as clearly as he could the stance we had taken and why.

The major studied him closely as he talked. "So you refuse to work as ordered. Is that right?"

"Yes, sir."

"That's all. Next man."

We were each questioned in like manner and then were made to stand a ways apart while the two officers again conferred quietly. I sensed that the uncertainty and fear was beginning to wear on each of us. The major picked up his roster and made a few quick notes, then turned to the door and left the brig.

The warden's voice was cold, but at least he'd stopped shouting. "Listen up and listen close. You prisoners are to be placed in solitary confinement in the cell block at the rear of the brig. You will have no privileges and you will remain so confined until further orders."

One by one we were then called by name to be taken to the cellblock. Alden was first. He was taken down the run to the back, shoved into the cell, and the lock was set with a sickening click.

Another chaser took Boundey. Too soon a chaser grabbed my arm, and I was escorted down that long walkway to the cell and shoved in. There wasn't enough cells for all 10 of us so the last three were returned to the cages, but spaced far apart.

★★

The cells were made from concrete blocks. There was a barred window in the door, and one high window on the side. A bunk was situated against the wall. The closed-in feeling was almost suffocating. This was much different from the open cages. My heart pounded against my ribs, and once again I struggled to make myself relax. After pacing for a time, I at last sat down on the bunk to rest. What a strange turn of events.

CHAPTER FOUR

I'd been shut up in the solitary cellblock for about 30 minutes when I heard a scuffling outside my cell door and the sound of the padlock clicking open. There stood a Marine lieutenant. I jumped up and stood at attention.

"At ease," the lieutenant said. "What's your name, sailor?"

"Pervis, Paul Harold."

"What's your rating?"

"Hospital apprentice, second class, sir."

"What are you in here for? What happened today? Why have you refused to work?"

My heart made a leap. Perhaps this officer had been sent to assess our situation and to work out an agreeable solution to this mess.

"Sir, it's a matter of conscience," I told him. Then I proceeded to explain to him our belief regarding the Sabbath of the Bible, and the reason that all of us felt we could not do what we had been asked to do.

"It's not up to you men to decide which work in the Navy is humanitarian and what is not," he countered. "Keeping up the grounds of this place is as necessary to the health and well-being of the sailors here as emptying bedpans."

When I heard those words, I realized he'd been sent to attempt to dissuade us. I had no way of knowing if my friends were now being talked to in the same manner. The lieutenant went on. "In my opinion, you men simply tried to get out of doing disagreeable work. It appears that you are just plain lazy."

"Sir, we are not lazy. We had no desire to get out of work. In fact, we asked that we be given double duty once the Sabbath was over at sundown this evening. We asked only that the work assigned us be delayed for a few hours."

My words fell on deaf ears as the lieutenant continued to try to wear me down. As he turned to go, the anger of his defeat was written on his stern face. "So you plan to stick with your decision?" His voice was low and hard. "Even if it means court-martial?"

Those dreaded words struck deep in the core of my being. "It's a matter of conscience with all of us," I repeated. "We have no alternative. The Bible clearly says—"

"Are you aware of where your disobedience might lead?"

"I suppose we might be sent to prison, sir."

"Sailor, have you ever heard of mutiny?"

"Yes, sir."

"Do you know what fate could be yours if you were to be charged and convicted of mutiny during wartime?"

My heartbeat thudded in my ears. "I think it's death."

"That's exactly right. I'd sure hate to see you men be so foolish as to continue this stupid religious nonsense and wind up before a firing squad."

At that point I could not answer. Nothing more could be said.

"If I were you, sailor, I'd give up these silly ideas before it's too late." The lieutenant stared at me hard and long. "For the last time I'm urging you personally and as a group to change your minds while there's still time. I'm in a position to know that the major is considering pursuing this case to the highest courts. Are you prepared for those consequences?"

He waited at the door, while I remained silent. "This is your last chance," he said. I still gave no answer. And with that, he went out the door.

Presently, I heard Buckley's hoarse whisper from the adjoining cell. "Pervis, who was that?"

"A Marine lieutenant."

"What'd he want?"

"Can't tell you now. Later. I can hardly hear—"

A booming voice from the front area cut off my words. "There'll be no whispering in the cellblock!" With that, all was quiet, except for the birdsongs sounding from the nearby jungle.

Time stood still as I sat there praying and wondering what might happen next. After a while, I heard Buckley begin to whistle a familiar hymn. I eagerly joined in. I heard yet another and another of our group joining the impromptu praise service. There was no retort from the guards, and that hymn did much to minister to the hearts of all of us.

It wasn't long before we were called out once again by Sergeant Kurzak's thundering voice shouting, "OK, you prisoners, prepare to line up at the black line." The clicking of padlocks being unlocked and doors opening echoed through the cellblock. A chaser accompanied us as we made our way to the black line in front of the warden's desk—in double time.

The fresh air in the walkway felt glorious after being shut up in the stuffy, humid cell. I wanted to drink in deep gulps of cool air. We were ordered to sound off, then led out the door and down the steps. "Form two columns and stand at *attention!*" the warden yelled from behind us.

When we had done so, the warden took his place at the

right front of the column. "Forward, march!"

We set out across the base, down several pathways, and around a number of buildings. The warden stopped us with a loud "Halt" outside what appeared to be the base head-quarters. We snapped to attention as we lined up on the walkway in front of the main entrance.

Out here, away from the closed-in brig, I grew acutely aware of the white "P" on my faded dungarees and of my shaved head. I felt the stares of others about us. We were in prison. We *looked* like prisoners.

The heat of the blazing afternoon sun burned relentlessly down on our bare heads. Hundreds of little hairs still scratched inside our shirts, and between that irritation and the tickle of trickling perspiration, it became a real chore to stand still.

"You there!" the chaser called to one of our guys in the rear of the line. "You call that being at attention? Straighten up, sailor." We all stood a little straighter.

The sun beat down, and sweat coursed down our backs and faces. Time inched slowly by. Five minutes, 10 minutes, 30 minutes. It became difficult to tell just how long we'd been standing there. Then in a sudden burst, the front door bolted open and a yeoman came out and spoke with the warden. The warden turned to the chaser. "Bring 'em in. The major will see them now."

We marched up the steps in our columns and were led through the door into Major MacArthur's office. "Stand here." The warden motioned where we were to line up single file, facing the major.

Several officers and yeomen stood about. Close beside the major's desk stood a lieutenant taking notes. I supposed him to be an attorney.

★★★★★★★★★★★★★★★★★★★★★★★★★★★★★★★★★★★★★★

The major's manner was cold and stern. "You men know why you are here?"

"Yes, sir," we answered almost in unison.

"You sailors have committed a very grave, a very serious offense. You have willingly disobeyed the lawful command of a superior officer in the line of duty—and *in time of war.*" The last words were stated slowly, precisely.

"You seem to have a perverted sense of religion. If I were you, I would expect to be *shot.*" The room was filled with an icy silence as the major paused for the full effect. "Your country is in a desperate struggle for survival. Any man who willingly disobeys the lawful order of a superior, acting in line of duty in wartime, does a disservice to his country, his comrades, and to himself. If you persist in this present action, I have no choice but to deal with this matter in the strictest way possible."

Then Major MacArthur put his hand on a stack of cigarettes and playing cards that lay on the corner of his desk. Slowly he scooted them to the middle of his desk. At that tense moment I had no way of knowing the significance of this act. It wasn't until later that I learned these items had been confiscated from four members of our group.

Evidently the major had been doing his homework. In addition to keeping the seventh-day Sabbath holy, Seventh-day Adventists neither smoke nor gamble. But cigarettes and cards had been found on four of our men. That must have been an agonizing moment for those four. Their actions had caught up with them.

The major didn't say anything. He just sat there with his hand near the stack of confiscated materials. After we had had the opportunity to assess what was happening, he continued. "Do any of you men have anything to say?"

I felt as though I couldn't breathe. Suddenly, to my complete surprise, one man said, "I do, sir. Privately, sir."

Our united front had now weakened. In a split second I had to make a heavy decision. If all nine others weakened and caved in, would I? While I searched deep inside my very soul, the major stood to his feet and escorted that sailor into a nearby room.

The heat was almost unbearable. The very air was brittle with tension. I had only a few minutes to come to grips with who I was, what I believed, and what I stood for. My decision to observe the Sabbath had not been made that morning, but many years before. I was standing in that place, not because of the other men, but because of what I knew in my heart to be truth. At that moment a gentle peace came over me and I rested in that. By the time the door opened and the major and the other prisoner returned, my struggle was settled.

The major returned to his desk, and the young man took his place back in the line. We had no way of knowing what he had said in that private consultation.

"Does anyone else have anything to say?" the major asked. There was silence. "Does anyone wish to go to work? If so, step forward." He paused, then added, "If you go to work right now, you will not be subject to a court-martial."

The man who had spoken with the major stepped forward, and a guard quickly ushered him out the door. The major asked the question one more time. "Does anyone wish to go to work?" As he did, three more of our group stepped forward and were taken away.

At a moment when my gut should have been wrenching, I was fine. I knew what I had to do.

The major spoke again. "Does anyone wish to go to work? If so, please step forward."

Despite this life-and-death question, the six of us stood quietly. No one moved.

"Very well then," Major MacArthur said. "I have no choice but to recommend you six men for a general court-martial. And you can be assured I will be seeking the stiffest penalty possible."

He turned to the warden. "My instructions are as follows: Return these men to the brig. Place two men to a cage. They are not to go out on any work detail. There is to be no communication between any of these six men or with the other prisoners. Each one must stay on his bunk continuously. They will have no reading material of any kind. No mail will be sent or received. That's all!"

My legs were weak with a strange sort of relief. The present crisis had passed.

"Prisoners!" It was the warden with the lungs once again. "Left face! Forward, march!"

We marched double time back to the brig. When we arrived at the steps, he shouted, "You will be split up two to a cage. You men are to spend all the rest of your time here sitting on your bunks. You will have nothing to read. You will not talk. You will not work. You will not exercise. You will sit from reveille to taps without moving, except to go to chow and to the head. Is that clear?"

"Yes, sir."

"I can't hear you, prisoners!"

"Yes, sir!"

"Chasers! Take these men to their cages." The chasers appeared at the door at the top of the stairs. "First man, up the stairs. *On the double!*"

It was Alden who ran up first. At the top of the stairs he was stopped, made to spread-eagle, and frisked. We hadn't been frisked the first time in, and we had changed clothes since then. But this was their ball game, and we certainly had no say-so.

One by one we were made to run up the stairs and then were frisked as we reached the door. As we went in, glasses were taken from those who wore them. Soon after, our Bibles were taken as well to ensure that the major's orders were carried out to the letter.

Alden and I were placed in the first cage, nearest the desk. We sat on our bunks as ordered. The threat of solitary confinement was never again mentioned, and I for one was deeply grateful. At least the cages were open and I could see out into the jungle beyond. It was now 1638, or 4:38 p.m.

We later learned that Sergeant Kurzak had been involved in some of the bloodiest fighting in the South Pacific. It was certainly understandable that he might hold contempt toward what he saw as shirkers. Especially when he had no understanding of our beliefs.

After a couple of hours, the sound of marching feet sounded from outside. The work detail was returning from the day's labor. Commands were shouted, and I realized then that Sergeant Kurzak yelled at every prisoner, not just us. In the heavy humidity of the brig, the stench of perspiration filled the air as the other prisoners came filing down the walkway and were let into the cages.

The four of our group who had gone to work were not separated from one another. But I noticed they kept their eyes averted as much as possible from the six of us. After the workers had cleaned up they were free to read or talk. We remained silently sitting on our bunks at rigid attention—arms folded, backs straight, feet on the floor, eyes straight ahead.

A whistle sounded, signaling chow time. The others

stood at attention, so we did likewise. The guard unlocked our cage and shouted the order: "Number one cage, up on the line." Alden and I joined our cell mates to rush to the black line in front of the warden's desk.

When all the prisoners were standing at attention we were made to run past the desk sounding off as we went. The first prisoners ran by yelling one after the other, "One," "Two," "Three . . ." But eventually someone would miss the count. The turnkey had us start all over. This routine might take as much as 20 minutes before we had it perfected. And we couldn't go to chow until it was perfect.

We double-timed to chow in single file with the chasers shouting at us all the way. The welcome aroma of food met us at the door of the chow hall. The first man double-timed to the far table, left-turned, rushed to the far end, turned again, and stood at attention behind the long wooden bench situated alongside the table.

Each man followed suit until the prisoners were standing at attention around the tables. When the warden was pleased with the formation and the quiet, he gave the command, "Prisoners, be seated." We stepped over the benches and settled in. Once again, when the warden felt it was quiet enough, a second command came: "Prisoners, commence eating."

As the others began digging in, I and my Adventist brothers bowed our heads to return thanks. I could feel the surprised stares of the others, but through the past months of being in the service, I'd grown accustomed to it.

The rule for prisoners in the chow hall was to sit rigidly at attention with arms folded when finished eating. To avoid that discomfort, we learned how to play around with the food until the very last minute. When everyone was finished, and it was quiet, another command was shouted: "Prisoners, rise!"

★★★

We stood at attention until we heard "Move out!" then double-timed single file back to the brig. Once we arrived, the warden announced that the "smoking lamp was lit." Those who smoked stayed outside for a time while the rest of us were frisked and returned to the cages.

Before lights out that evening, the warden came down the walkway and said in his booming voice, "Six new prisoners were brought in today. Their offense is none of your business. Do not talk to them, do not look at them, do not have anything to do with them. You are to pretend they are not even here. That is an order."

That order was a rather thin one, since it only served to pique the curiosity of the other men. Soon our situation was well known in the entire brig.

I can never remember being as thankful to lie down on an old wooden bunk as I was when darkness finally fell that night. But sleep was a long time coming. So many voices had bombarded me through the course of the long day. Now all of them echoed in my brain. So many accusations. So much misunderstanding. I almost had to smile as I remembered the accusation of being lazy. I'd been called a few things in my life, but lazy had never been among them. As far back as I could remember, my life had been filled with long days of hard work.

CHAPTER FIVE

On October 13, 1906, my father, George Barton Pervis, took Maud Lenora Craig to be his wife, in Palm View, Manatee County, Florida. In 1912 they moved to Sneads Island, a small island on the Manatee River. Some of the first orange groves in the Orlando area were planted by my grandfather on Dad's side. The roots of the Pervises sink deep into the warm, rich soil of the Sunshine State.

In Manatee County, my father began farming a rather impressive amount of acreage, producing a wide variety of vegetables in season. As a young farmer and businessman, Dad was known throughout the area for his fairness and the good wages he paid.

Woodrow Wilson was elected president that year, thousands of Americans flocked to the new "cinemas," and the grand ocean liner, the *Titanic,* collided with an iceberg and sank during her maiden voyage. However, few of those far-reaching matters were of interest to Maud and Barton Pervis. A much more important issue affecting them was that Florida was catching up with California in becoming the fruit- and vegetable-producing capital of the nation. Raising produce and rearing boys became their prime occupation for a number of years.

My four strapping older brothers were born in quick

order: Emory in 1908, Irvin in 1910, Laurence in 1912, and Arthur in 1916. The busy Pervis household was bursting at the seams.

In 1917 Dad ordered lumber to be brought in by boat from Tampa, and he built a sturdy two-story frame house near the bank of the river. Two years later, in the downstairs bedroom of the new home, Maud gave birth to a fifth son, me—Paul Harold. It had been three years since the birth of her last child, and my mother was overjoyed at having yet another babe in her arms.

After the older boys completed morning chores and went off to school each day, Mother and I spent many contented hours together. As I grew older, a close bond formed between the two of us. One day as Mother sat with her head bent over her intricate embroidery work, I began to pester her. "Let me help. Let me make flowers," I insisted. I remember being fascinated with her beautiful intricate stitches and the resulting detailed artwork.

"You want to embroider like this?" She held up the pillowcase where at one end her embroidery hoops circled the pink and lavender flowers she was stitching.

"Yes, yes," came my excited reply. "Let me try."

So Mother stopped her work and took a clean piece of cloth and with a pencil drew a series of flowers. She took another set of embroidery hoops and stretched the cloth taut. She then began to teach her youngest son to embroider with the same bright colorful thread that she used. As my family told it, I took to the work quickly and easily. Perhaps in today's society, I might have been called a "sissy." Later, however, my hands would knit casting nets to use for fishing in the Manatee River.

Another one of my early jobs was to help clean the

kerosene lamps that gave us light each night. The lamps not only needed cleaning but refilling, and the wicks trimmed. Although the light was poor, I remember Dad reading for long hours in the evening by the lamp's soft glow.

On wash day Mother built a fire under the black cast-iron wash pot in the backyard. I used my knife to cut small pieces of P&G soap into the boiling water. Sometimes I helped stir the clothes with a stick, which helped loosen the dirt. Doing laundry was a day-long process.

It wasn't long before I was given more industrious chores to perform. I milked the cows, gathered eggs, and fed the animals. Since our produce fields were vital to our living, I was also taught to carefully weed the seed beds that held the seedlings for Dad's massive farming operations. Later, I learned to set the plants out in the field in rows. Those rows, in my childlike mind, were at least 10 miles long. Dad showed me precisely how far apart to space the vegetables: peppers were set 12 inches apart, while eggplants were set three feet apart. Planting time meant especially long days for the Pervis men.

There was always ample work to do, whether hoeing off acres to prepare for planting or doing the planting itself. Growing crops had to be fertilized. Weeding, it seemed, never ended.

My father set a superb example of work ethics for all five of his sons. He worked the farm from daylight to dark, and often late into the night—working by the flickering light of a lantern set atop an upturned hamper. Dad was a small wiry man, never weighing more than 150 pounds. Yet, many times I saw him take a 200-pound bag of fertilizer from the truck, sling it up on his back, and stride across a plowed field.

In the tropical heat of the Florida summer, when few

crops could be grown, Dad resorted to deep-sea fishing. He was relentless in his determination to provide for his family.

The waterway that separated Sneads Island from the mainland was called the "cutoff," or "cut" for short, and it was much wider when I was a boy than in later years. At that time a skiff ferried people and wagons across the cut. I remember going to town with Dad on business. On the return trip, Dad would drop off to sleep and the horse would take us home without guidance from anyone.

The Manatee River was an integral part of our lives. Fishing, swimming, and boating were daily events. Sometimes in the night hours, Mother would awaken to the sounds of fish jumping. She'd get up and go to the river. With expert dexterity, she flung her cast nets into the river and brought in fish for a family meal.

My brothers and I delighted in making boats and playing with them along the riverbanks. Floating the boats and pushing them along with sticks was great sport for young boys who had no other entertainment. On one particular day when the older boys were away at school, I begged to go down to the river and play with my sailboat.

"No," Mother told me. "Stay close to the house. There's no one to go to the river to watch over you."

Determined in my search for a place to float my little boat, I found the perfect "pond"—the rain barrel. Since I was accustomed to climbing trees, crawling up on a rain barrel was no challenge. Indeed there was water—it was nearly half full. But it was a great stretch for my short arms to place my boat in the water. Suddenly, with a loud splash I fell in headfirst. Had Mother not heard the noise and come to investigate, I surely would have drowned. Although it was a frightening experience, it never squelched my love for the river or for playing in water.

Mother was a splendid cook and kept our table laden with such delicacies as grapefruit-rind candy, lemon pie, banana cake, guava cobbler, guava jelly, and sea grape jelly. We boys delighted to come home from school to a treat of syrup cake. Breakfasts, consisting of rice and tomato gravy, eggs, pure cane syrup, and hot biscuits spread with home-churned butter, kept Maud's hardworking menfolk healthy and hearty.

But her culinary skills were not limited to feeding the family. Anyone who visited our home was enticed to stay for a meal. Mother enjoyed people, and doted on visiting guests.

Even though we didn't have all that much to spare, Mother's unselfish heart made certain any underprivileged neighbor children had gifts at Christmas, as well as her own five. I often marveled in later years as I thought back and remembered her openhearted generosity.

Another of Mother's skills was in the role of family social director, as she constantly organized lively outings. On a moment's notice she was planning a picnic or a fish fry. Being a fun-loving person, she never waited for a holiday—berry picking time was a good excuse for a picnic or a party.

Dad's brother was a light keeper at a lighthouse on a barrier island, Egmont Key. Mother would gather her sisters and their families, hire a boat to transport us all, and head to the island for day-long picnics. All of the cousins spent hours of playtime together clamming, swimming, or even spur-of-the-moment baseball games.

During that time we were surrounded by families who were Seventh-day Adventists, and that had a profound effect upon my family. One summer my three older brothers traveled to Pennsylvania and worked at an Adventist camp meeting. When they returned home they were ignited with zeal for the church. This, too, affected the family. They were persuaded that since God rested on the seventh day of Creation week, Christians should observe the Sabbath and keep it holy. The fourth commandment, they felt, was a further admonition that they should rest from work on the seventh day—Saturday. For a time, I even attended a local Seventh-day Adventist church school.

In 1929 the peace and tranquillity of my safe little world was forever destroyed. Mother, always sympathetic and caring, fretted over a newborn calf and went out in the cold rain to tend to it. Years later I realized her physical condition was probably weakened by her load of hard work, and thus she became susceptible to illness. Chilled by the cold and rain, she contracted bronchial pneumonia.

She was ill for a number of days before she was finally taken to a hospital in Orlando. When she was placed in the neighbor's car to leave, she turned to me and said softly, "Harold, I'll never see you again." Those words broke my young heart. I never did see her again, for she died a few days later at age 42. I was only 10 years old.

Our household was forever changed, but the sunlight of Mother's tenderness and love never left us. My gentle father and my doting older sisters-in-law helped to ease the pain of my deep sense of loss.

Following Mother's death, Dad and I shared the household chores. I learned how to make biscuits and Dad got the process of making guava jelly down to a fine art. But the anchor who'd held our family together and organized so many spirited social events was gone. I had not only lost a parent, but a dear friend. Mother had always taken time to talk to me, and I missed her terribly.

Eventually Dad made plans to move to Fort Myers to

farm, but for various reasons, the effort fell through. Instead, he moved across the bay to Palma Sola, where I attended fifth through the tenth grades. That first spring an unexpected tidal wave wiped out all the vegetable plants, the saltwater killing them on contact. It was a time of struggle and disappointment for our entire family.

Since there were no girls in our family, we boys had always been taught by Mother to wash and iron the clothes. The heavy irons were heated on the stove, used until they cooled, then traded for a hot one again. There were no insulated handles as irons have today, and they could only be held with a thick padded mat.

This was a tiring process and I hated the job, especially in the summer. One summer my uncle was staying with us and he kindly asked me to iron a pair of his trousers. Later, he told my father that when I ironed the trousers, he had three creases in each leg!

Previous to Mother's passing, our family had joined the Seventh-day Adventist church in Palmetto, and following her death, Dad continued to take us to Sabbath school and church each Saturday in the old farm truck. Many of my young friends also attended the church. It was a time of growing friendships.

By age 14 my responsibilities on the farm had greatly increased. I was given the job of driving our truck to Tampa to market during harvesttime. During this busy season the market ran 24 hours a day. While one of the older boys stayed at the market, my job was to return home to take another load out. It was vital that the highly perishable produce reach the market quickly. Sometimes we went days with little or no sleep, catching quick catnaps whenever we could. A boy grows up fast when shouldering that kind of responsibility.

Eventually, one of my brothers launched out in the produce business. He handled Dad's crops and sold our vegetables. This was more lucrative than working with the packinghouses.

By the time I was in high school, it was obvious there would be no money to send me to college, but I learned of a Seventh-day Adventist boarding school in Collegedale, Tennessee, called Southern Junior College. The school offered the opportunity for students to work their way through. Both high school and junior college curriculum were provided on the same campus. The place seemed right for me. Since I'd worked hard all my life, working my way through college would be no different. I began saving my money and making plans to go.

Before time to leave, my sister-in-law, Danie, took me on a day-long shopping spree in Tampa. She helped me choose the clothes I'd need in the cooler climate. Together we picked out curtains, bedspreads, and rugs for my dorm room. Although she wasn't much older than I, Danie willingly stepped in as my mother figure.

Danie and I were at a department store where I was trying on clothes. I came out of the dressing room in my spiffy new slacks and shirt and stood before the full-length mirror. I was now five feet ten, taller than most of my brothers, and much taller and more broad-shouldered than Dad. Danie sat off to the side, studying me. At length, she said, "Harold, if Maud Pervis had lived, she would be mighty proud of you today."

As I lay quietly in my bunk in the Trinidad Navy Brig, my memories of home and family brought waves of homesickness over me like none I'd experienced since first being inducted. The uncertainties that lay ahead filled me with a sick, frightening feeling. But once again, my special verse came to my mind, *"The angel of the Lord encampeth round about them that fear him, and delivereth them."* The word "deliver" spoke to my spirit, and I finally drifted off to sleep on the uncomfortable bunk.

CHAPTER SIX

✦

The next morning I was jolted awake at 0600 to the squawking sounds of reveille played on a scratchy much-used record, and blasted over a bullhorn that hung just outside the brig.

Dressing quickly, I glanced down the way at the other prisoners in the cages. What a dreadful reminder of our situation. *With my shaved head and wrinkled dungarees, I'm totally indistinguishable from the other prisoners,* I thought with a shock. *And some of them have committed violent crimes.*

We were taken to chow, then led back and placed into our cages. The other prisoners were organized into work details and taken out to work. As on the previous day, our four SDA brothers who'd chosen to work Saturday avoided any eye contact with us. If I envied their activity, perhaps they envied my peace of mind. I was more convinced than ever that we'd done the right thing according to our beliefs.

We had now begun the first day of the strange sentence—to spend the entire day sitting or lying on our bunks. Remaining totally idle was something entirely foreign to me. By the time the first two hours had crept by, I longed to jump up and do 50 jumping jacks. Or just talk to my buddies. We were able to sneak a wink, or a flicker of a smile to one another now and then.

I thought noon chow time would never arrive, but at long last we heard the pounding footsteps of the work detail coming our way. We ate as ravenously as the men who had been hacking away at the jungle all morning, eating everything except the meat and refusing the coffee and tea. Much too soon we were marched back to our cages, where the workers were allowed a few brief minutes of rest. Those in our little group, however, were quickly placed back in the cages, and the rigid no-talking rule was once again enforced. I had only thought the morning was long. The afternoon became much worse.

The heat from the tropical afternoon sunshine was heavy in the brig, and my full stomach made me extremely sleepy. I knew if I slept the afternoon away, I'd lie awake all night.

As the afternoon dragged by, Montgomery suddenly jumped up and trotted double time to the black line.

"Where do you think you're going?" the turnkey demanded.

"Sir, I need to go to the head."

The turnkey looked at him for a moment. "Make it fast!"

"Yes, sir. Thank you, sir." Montgomery raced toward the head.

After only a few minutes, the turnkey shouted, "You've been in there long enough. Get back to that bunk *on the double.*"

I heard sounds of shuffling from the head, and soon Montgomery came racing back to his cage. I cringed, knowing my time would come before long.

I soon learned how to use mental exercises. I attempted to go through the entire multiplication tables, and not miss one. If I stumbled on one, I made myself go back to the first and begin again. Bible verses also helped as I searched my brain to try to remember as many as I could, trying to say them to myself word for word. Verses of hymns were done the same way. As I went over the lyrics of a few of my favorites, I found they held fresh new meaning, and I felt my spirit being edified.

I'm not sure who was most thankful for lights out that night, the prisoners whose backs ached from the grueling work or the six of us who ached all over from doing nothing. As I fell asleep the second night, I found myself dreading the dawn.

The next day was a replica of the former. Each minute dragged out interminably long. The mornings were somewhat cooler, but the afternoons were long, hot, and wearisome. Our full stomachs from the noon meal made us extremely sleepy in the hot afternoon.

At every meal the six of us left the meat portions untouched, since we were strict vegetarians. To our surprise, at one evening chow the six of us were seated at a separate table. On our table sat a variety of splendidly prepared meat dishes, along with bread, coffee, and water. We quickly understood that someone had been doing their homework about the beliefs and practices of Seventh-day Adventists, and that this was a test.

After bowing our heads to thank God for our food, we ate only the bread and drank only the water. None of us knew but what this would be repeated at every meal from then on, but thankfully it happened only once. Perhaps they were beginning to see that our beliefs were not a pastime with us, but part and parcel of our lives. Needless to say, that night when we lay down in our bunks our stomachs were still quite empty.

By the third day we discovered that the rotating turnkeys cared very little about enforcing our sentence to the letter. We became increasingly aware that they chose to ignore minor infractions. Naturally, the more they ignored, the more we tried to do. We were able to communicate with motions and expressions. This helped some to pass the time. We learned later that word had passed among the turnkeys that we were not going to cause any trouble for them.

On Wednesday we were surprised when a young Navy lieutenant came to visit us. This tall fellow introduced himself as Lieutenant Slaght, and said he wanted to talk to us. When we were gathered together into one cage, he asked a number of questions about our treatment and the unique beliefs that had led to our incarceration. I, for one, was pleased that this officer had come to gain a better understanding of our predicament. Evidently I was not alone, for each one of our group freely and honestly answered all his questions.

Later that day we learned, to our dismay, that this man was none other than the judge advocate who was assigned to preside at our court-martial trial. We all felt sick at this news, for it seemed we'd been purposely tricked. After that, we were wary of anyone and everyone who was not part of the regular brig routine.

The previous Saturday when we'd been arrested at the hospital, word had spread like wildfire, and James Riggs quickly got wind of it. By investigative follow-up, he learned the details about our situation. Since he was closely acquainted with Gracie and me, he wrote Gracie a letter to let her know what had happened and promised he would stay in touch.

But James didn't stop there. He immediately visited the local SDA pastors in Port of Spain and apprised them of the situation. W. E. Read served as president of the Caribbean Union Conference, and C. J. Ritchie, as president of the South Caribbean Conference. These two men lent a sympathetic ear to James's story.

★★★★★★★★★★★★★★★★★★★★★★★★★★★★★★★★★★★★★

So it was that on Thursday we saw a man dressed in civilian clothes, accompanied by a Navy shore patrolman, come into the brig and stop at the desk of the turnkey. Since I was closest to the desk, I heard the patrolman say that this man had permission to see the prisoners. As usual, we were the only ones in the brig, since the work detail was out.

The turnkey brought the visitor to the first cage, where Alden and I were kept, then the others were brought to join us. Having been previously tricked by a seemingly sympathetic visitor, we eyed this civilian with great suspicion, even though he seemed friendly and sported a warm smile.

When the turnkey and the patrolman returned to the office area, the man announced, "I'm Pastor C. J. Ritchie. I'm with the SDA mission here in Trinidad."

None of us could believe this stroke of good fortune. Finally something was turning in our favor. After a round of friendly hand shaking and name exchanging we were able to sit on the bunks and visit. He explained how James Riggs and another sailor had visited the conference office to relay what had happened. I would forever feel indebted to Riggs for taking the time, trouble, and effort to get the word out to the place where we could receive the most help—our local church.

We were inspired by Pastor Ritchie's visit, by his counsel, advice, and prayers. After the letdown from being deceived by the young Lieutenant Slaght, we now had a true friend in our corner. I lay down to sleep that night with a tiny new thread of hope to hang on to.

The judge advocate returned the next day for a second visit. This time there was no facade—he was all business. He had come to provide us with a copy of the charge and specifications upon which we were to be tried. He read the document aloud, and we followed along. The charge stated that

we had "jointly" disobeyed a lawful order. This could be mis-
construed to be *mutiny*. At this, I felt a stab of panic. We
would face a general court-martial, which is the highest
court-martial that the Navy conducts.

"Do you wish for the Navy to provide counsel to repre-
sent you?" the lieutenant asked after he finished reading.

By this point, we were fairly distrustful of anyone in the
military, but not one of us had any experience in legal matters. Finally Buckley spoke up. "Sir, we decline counsel, and
request only that Pastor C. J. Ritchie, from the Seventh-day
Adventist church of Port of Spain, be present."

"Are all of you agreed on this matter?"

The lieutenant looked at each of us. We assured him we
were agreed. I didn't see that we had any other options.
"Very well," he said. Then he asked if any one of us desired
to make a statement at that time. We did not. "Court date,"
the lieutenant informed us, "is set for Monday, 2 October,
1944, at 0900." Having said that, he turned and left.

We had much to think and pray about, and many long
hours to wait through until Monday morning.

That evening after the work detail had returned, Major
MacArthur came by on one of his weekly visits to the brig.
He asked if we had any requests.

"Yes, sir," I spoke up quickly. "May we have our Bibles
and eyeglasses returned?"

The major looked surprised, and quickly called for the
warden to come forward. "Did you order the Bibles to be
taken from these men?" he asked.

"Sir, you ordered that there was to be no reading material."

"I've never yet refused a prisoner his right to have a Bible.
Return to these men their Bibles and glasses."

The burly Sergeant Kurzak saluted and gave a snappy,

"Yes, sir," while I and my buddies gave a collective silent cheer and exchanged smiles of encouragement. How good it was to finally have something to do! We each began to soak up God's word during the quiet endless hours while sitting on our bunks.

Without fail, each one of us knelt by our bunks to pray before retiring at night. One evening as we did so, a guard called out, "You boys better be praying. It's gonna take more than prayer to get you out of this mess." Then he called another guard to come and watch this spectacle. We ignored their taunts and their laughter. And we continued kneeling down to pray each night.

As the weekend hours crawled by, our foreboding about Monday's trial grew. We had no way of knowing what might happen. Another visit from Pastor Ritchie on Sabbath afternoon broke up the boredom. During this time, with the pastor's kind help, the six of us drew up a statement to present at our trial. We decided to rest our case entirely on the matter of freedom of religion and of conscience, and nothing else. Whether it would help us or harm us, we had no way of knowing.

At breakfast Monday morning, we could only pick at the scrambled eggs on our plates. We hardly dared to look at one another, dreading to see the nervousness mirrored in our faces. We were back on our bunks and waiting by 0800. Since the trial was scheduled for 0900, we assumed they would come to get us at least by half past eight.

A gnawing of fear and dread tied knots in my belly. I paged through the book of Psalms in my Bible, and repeatedly read my favorite promise, Psalm 34:7. The word "deliver" held more and greater meaning for me.

Each time the turnkey rattled his newspaper I jumped,

thinking someone was coming for us. At last, we heard the sounds of boots crunching on the gravel in the walkway outside. I placed my Bible at the foot of my bunk as the turnkey shouted, "You six men, up on the line on the double." Surprisingly, there was no threatening anger in his voice this morning. "Sound off as you come by."

We ran past the desk shouting our numbers in perfect order, and were stopped at the foot of the stairs by a group of spit-and-polish shore patrolmen formed into two columns. We fell in between those columns, after which the lead patrolman shouted, "Forward, *march!*"

This was it. We were on our way.

The morning was unbelievably clear and shining. The dark green of the jungle palms fringing the base contrasted against the soft blue of the tropical skies. Melodic songs of the tropical birds accompanied us as we marched along. The gentle breezes playing in the palm fronds seemed to mock the tight knot forming in my gut.

Officers and enlisted men passing us on the walkway cast a curious eye in our direction. We were unaware, but our trial was the talk of the entire base. The patrolmen led us to the headquarters building, where we were met by another patrolman at the door. "Bring the men right in," he said.

We moved into the building and stood at attention in the hallway. It took a few moments for our eyes to adjust from the brilliant sunshine to the darker interior. Directly before us a pair of large double doors opened to reveal a makeshift courtroom. Personnel scurried about the hallway like busy little ants. Presently, I caught sight of Lieutenant Slaght striding somberly toward the open double doors. He whisked past us without so much as a nod.

Just before time to go in, Pastor Ritchie arrived. Our spirits were lifted by his presence and friendly smile. At precisely 0900 a guard came to the door. "This way, men."

With our pastor at our side, we marched inside. The room was vast; bright sunshine streamed through its open windows. However, no amount of sun could chase the stiff, cold atmosphere from the place.

The room bore no resemblance to a civilian courtroom. A long table was positioned in the center of the room. Sitting at the table was a row of seven officers, all sporting plenty of gold braid, and shining medals. Two were commanders, three were lieutenant commanders, and two were lieutenants. Besides those at the table, provost marshals, orderlies, and reporters were present. A grave, solemn group to be sure.

Facing the officers' table was another table with seven empty chairs. We were told to be seated there, and Pastor Ritchie sat at our far left. As we were pulling out chairs and sitting down, I could feel all the eyes studying us. I'm sure we must have appeared as a strange group to these rigid, military-trained officers.

In a stand behind the officers' table, our nation's glorious stars and stripes hung gracefully from its pole. I couldn't help marveling at the paradox of this entire scenario. There hung our flag, which stands for freedom of worship. Here were professional officers who were actively fighting to preserve that very freedom. And before them sat six men who were being tried for having exercised that freedom. It didn't make much sense.

CHAPTER SEVEN

T he room was deathly still as Judge Advocate Lieutenant Slaght stood to introduce the court by name and rank. He then called each of our names and asked if we had any objections to anyone on the court. None of us did. We were then asked if we had received a copy of the charge and the specifications upon which we were to be tried. As our names were called we answered in the affirmative. Following this we were asked if we had objections to make to the charge and specifications. This time we each answered in the negative.

These were the preliminaries, and once they were out of the way a short recess was called. The recess served only to set our nerves more on edge. As we reconvened, court was now duly called to order, and we were each asked separately if we were ready for the trial—as though we could ever be ready. Each man replied, "Yes, sir."

The charge and specifications were read by the judge advocate, and then came the question: "Vesterlide S. Alden, hospital apprentice second class, U.S. Navy inductee, you have heard the charge and specifications preferred against you; how say you to the first specification of the charge, guilty or not guilty?"

Alden's clear voice rang out through the cavernous room as he stood and spoke the words "Guilty, sir."

I felt I would choke through my dry throat, but when my turn came, I also spoke loud and clear. "Guilty, sir."

The process was repeated as the second specification was read. We were then warned of the possible effect that our pleas might have on the trial's outcome, but we stood by our previous statements.

Now Alden rose to read the statement that we had prepared with the pastor's guidance and counsel:

We, the undersigned enlisted men, deeply regret the incident which has occurred. We desire to reaffirm our loyalty and pledge of allegiance to our government and officers and to Captain Tabor and Major MacArthur in particular.

We sincerely regret that on or about 23 September, 1944, we could not and did not obey Captain Tabor's order to take an outside work detail on the day we observe as the Sabbath of God. For the same reason we could not and did not obey the command of Major MacArthur to go to work with the prison work detail on the same day. We desire to assure the court that our attitude is one of obedience and full submission to all lawful authority. All we respectfully request is that we be permitted to observe the Sabbath (from sundown Friday to sundown Saturday) in a manner in harmony with the requirements of God and the religious beliefs of the Seventh-day Adventist Church of which we are members. This does not mean we are presumptuously asking to be always relieved of all duties on the Sabbath Day, for we are perfectly willing to do our full part by doing such duties as are in harmony with God's Sabbath Law, for example bedside nursing, ministering to the sick and wounded.

We further respectfully request that the provisions of the Navy Sabbath Order and of Bureau of Naval Personnel Circular Letter No. 115-43 with reference to the bona fide religious beliefs

*and convictions of Navy personnel be put into early effect in this
base, so as to avoid placing us in these unfavorable situations in
the future.*

He then read off all our names, as we had each signed this
statement. We were asked individually if we were in agreement with the statement. All of us affirmed that we were indeed in agreement. Following this, it was time to proceed
with the interrogation of the witnesses for the prosecution.

Grounds Master at Arms Martin was the first to be called.
He was asked if he recognized us as part of a group who reported to him for duty on the morning of 23 September, 1944.
He acknowledged that we were part of that group. When
asked if difficulties arose that morning, MA Martin said, "One
man asked me how he could get out of work on Saturday."

"Tell us in your own words what happened."

"I told him to go see the chief master at arms. There were
more who didn't want to work on Saturday, so I formed this
group and took them up to the chief master at arms."

I felt my heart sinking. It never occurred to any of us that
they might simply present us as a group attempting to get
out of work on Saturday. Surely none of these officers would
believe that.

Chief Master at Arms Howland was next to be questioned. His interpretation of the situation was similar to
Martin's.

"What did the outside master at arms tell you?" the
judge asked.

"He told me that they had approached him with the
statement that they would not work on Saturday. He then
brought them to me."

"At that time, did you explain to these men the work routine of the hospital?" came the next question.

"I did."

"Did you give them a direct order to go to work?"

"I did."

"What was that order?"

"I directed them to go to work with the outside work detail."

"What was their reply?"

"They said they could not and would not go to work."

The judge paused momentarily as though for effect. "Did you at that time ask them if they wished to talk it over among themselves?"

Howland's voice was clear and steady in the large room. "They said they had already talked it over among themselves and they did not wish to carry out this order."

"In other words, they told you that they had discussed their refusal to obey this order among themselves?"

"Yes, sir."

I fought to keep from squirming in my chair. This was beginning to sound more and more like a planned mutiny. I was astonished at the direction the trial was taking and how easily we were misunderstood.

At this point, Buckley and Montgomery both asked questions that were aimed to clarify our stand that morning. But Howland stated he "didn't recall the situation as they referred to it."

I was surprised at the short memories of these men.

Commander Vaughn was next on the stand. He was asked about the schedules for the hospital, to which he replied it was run on a seven-day workweek. The irony of this questioning was in the fact that if we had been assigned to work in the hospital, carrying out humanitarian efforts, the ensuing incident would never have occurred.

He was then asked about the chapel and if Seventh-day Adventists used the chapel, and he explained that SDA sailors have permission to use the chapel every Friday evening.

From this line of questioning they then moved back to the morning in question. "Commander, on the morning of 23 September, 1944, did there come a time when the accused and four other men were brought before you by the master at arms?"

"Yes, sir."

"What did he tell you?"

"He stated that he had 10 men who refused to obey the orders of the outside master at arms and refused to work."

"What did you do then?"

"I instructed the chief master at arms to bring the 10 men to my office. I then ordered those 10 men to obey the orders and to go to work. They left the office without making any comment."

At that point, Boundey asked again about our request for the day off, as opposed to blatantly disobeying an order. To which the commander answered, "No mention was made of having a day off."

When Captain Tabor was questioned, the judge used the same line, asking if the hospital was on a seven-day workweek, and if the Seventh-day Adventist personnel used the chapel. I couldn't see how that detail had any bearing on what had happened.

When asked to explain what happened the captain answered, "This group of men was brought in at 0945 on the morning of 23 September, 1944. I asked them if they refused to perform their duties, and they said they did. They refused to perform any unnecessary work. I explained to them that it was not within their province to determine what work was necessary or unnecessary at the hospital, and in refusing to perform their work they were committing a serious offense."

The captain then explained that he brought us into mast, and since we still had "refused to obey," as he put it, he sentenced us to five days in the Marine Brig of the Naval Operating Base.

Now it was our turn. Boundey asked the captain if he knew when we were brought before him that we were Seventh-day Adventists, to which the captain answered yes.

He then asked the captain if to his knowledge any of our group had ever disobeyed any lawful order given by a superior officer before this incident. But Captain Tabor quickly avoided this by saying since we were new to the base he had no knowledge of our previous actions.

I then stood and asked, "Sir, do you remember I asked you for the day off under the Navy regulation providing for personnel having the Sabbath day off so that we might observe religious services?"

This time I was not shocked when he simply answered, "I don't recall the incident." This evidently was going to be their standard reply. How convenient for them. I sat down feeling as though I'd had the wind knocked out of me.

Marine Sergeant Kurzak was called next. He explained how Alden, Boundey, and Buckley had been sent out to work. "What happened next?" the judge wanted to know.

"They were brought before me because they refused to work."

"Did they state to you their reason for refusing to work?"

"I didn't ask them. The work I asked them to do was grounds maintenance."

"Are all prisoners required to work?"

"Those who do not work are those on bread and water, and those in solitary confinement."

"What happened next?"

"At that time the chaser ordered each man to go to work individually and they all refused."

"What did you do upon their refusal?" the judge asked.

"I called Major MacArthur."

As one witness followed another, the room grew warmer and warmer. Tiny beads of sweat were forming on my face and slowly trickling down. An oscillating fan droned in the corner, but none of its breeze reached us.

During Major MacArthur's questioning, he was asked about religious services offered in the brig. "No provision is made," he explained, "except that chaplains are permitted free access to the brig. I've never had a request from a prisoner to attend services."

When asked to explain what happened, he told how he had questioned each of us separately, and that we all refused to work. "I asked them why they refused to obey, and they said individually that they refused to obey his orders because it was against their religion to do any but necessary work on Saturday. I asked them who was to determine what work was necessary. They said they reserved the right to so determine what work was necessary."

I marveled that this story was growing stranger and stranger. None of us had ever said we reserved the right to determine what work was necessary on the base. But we had offered to work double duty after sundown or on Sunday. That, however, was never mentioned.

"Major," the judge asked, "would it have been possible for you to let these men off for the entire day of Saturday without any work?"

"Yes," answered the major. "However, I am required by my orders to work prisoners."

"If you should have decided to let them off on Saturday, could you have worked them on Sunday?"

"Yes, sir. But it would have been necessary to keep a full guard on all day Sunday." From there he proceeded to explain how Sunday afternoons were liberty for all guards and chasers.

After the major had been questioned, Lieutenant Brown, from the legal office, was called. I recognized him as being the one who stood by in the major's office. At one point, the lieutenant was asked, "Did you hear Major MacArthur make any criticism of the accused's religious beliefs?"

"At no time did he criticize them," answered Lieutenant Brown.

When Alden stood to cross-examine, he asked, "Sir, do you remember when Major MacArthur told us we might get a general court-martial—do you remember the major saying we had a perverted sense of religion?"

As expected, the lieutenant replied, "No, I don't remember that. As far as I know, he didn't make any statement outside of explaining his own position."

There was no further questioning of this lieutenant, and he was asked to step down.

With a few more formalities, court concluded and the room was cleared. The other prisoners were as stunned as I was. My heart was heavy as we were returned to the brig. It was as though we'd been talking to the wind all that time. Not one of the officers had heard us.

It didn't take much to understand that things didn't look well for us.

Lying on the hard bunk that night, I couldn't stop thinking about Gracie and little Paul. If my pay was cut, how would they make it? While I was sure Gracie would agree totally with my actions, still I fought the feeling of having let her down. My tiny little Gracie was the best thing that had ever happened to me. And to think if I hadn't decided as a young teen to attend Southern Junior College, we might have never met.

CHAPTER EIGHT

I arrived at the campus of Southern Junior College in the fall of 1936. This unique school was the brainchild of an SDA minister, Pastor Colcard, who as early as 1894 saw the need for educating and training young Adventists for missionary work. The church liked the idea of an "industrial school" where work and study were combined.

In 1916 the school ownership transferred to the local conference of the Adventist Church, and the campus moved to its present location near Chattanooga, Tennessee. The village was given the name of Collegedale by an SDA evangelist, Carlyle B. Haynes. (This man was to have a great effect on my life in later years.)

The school was spread across the side of a hill, affording a splendid view down into the valley. Two large well-built dormitories anchored each end of the campus. The administrative and classroom buildings were tucked in between.

The town consisted of one general store, a dairy, a broom shop, a woodcraft shop, a printing plant, a hosiery mill, and, of course, Southern Junion College. I signed a three-year contract to work at the hosiery mill while I attended school. My wages not only paid my tuition, but also put a few dollars in my pocket each week for spending money.

Not many students opted for the work-study program because it allowed no breaks for employees to take a home leave. The contract stated that work-study students be employed straight through the summer months as well as the school year. Few students were willing to sacrifice occasional visits home to work there.

In January of that year, a new student arrived on campus from Mississippi—a petite personable girl by the name of Gracie Beaube. She caught my attention immediately, but between my long work hours, study time, and strict campus rules forbidding much contact between the sexes—not to mention my own terrible shyness—nothing much happened for a time.

Gracie signed up for the work-study program and therefore worked at the hosiery mill with me. At least I got to see her there.

High school students attended classes in the morning, working at the mill from 1:30 to 9:30 p.m. The work was tedious and painstaking. Gracie began as a "topper," working on the machine that formed the foot of the silk stocking. Because it was piecework, she was required to finish several pieces every few minutes without dropping a stitch. The toppers sat down to stitch, then jumped up again to place their pieces on a larger machine, where the feet were completed. The job called for energetic, attentive workers.

I, on the other hand, was at the knitting machines, where eighteen hose were knitted at a time. It required a constant vigil: watching that the spools didn't wind off, changing bad needles, taking care that each new needle was placed in straight, and at the same time minding the stitch counter. The work kept me running up and down the line of machines for eight hours.

In spite of long hours of work and study, we had opportunity for fun. The school planned various functions and outings, such as boating, swimming and picnics. Eventually, I gathered my nerve and when an outing approached, I'd ask Gracie, "Do you want to go with me?" She always said yes.

Strict school rules kept the girls separated from the boys during chapel, and no boys were allowed to even walk a girl to her dormitory door. However, the school allowed what were called "parlor dates" at the girls' dorm. The boys were allowed to come in and sit in the small "parlor" with their girlfriends and talk—and maybe even sneak a kiss or two. Even these dates were limited to only one hour per week.

When I graduated from high school in 1938, my brother, Laurence and his wife, Danie, attended my graduation ceremony. Danie, ever the mother-type, was concerned about my social life.

"Harold," she asked, "don't you have a girlfriend?"

Pointing to Gracie, I said, "See that girl over there?"

Danie turned to see my petite Gracie with her bright eyes and bubbly personality. "Yes?" she said, expecting some good news.

I gave a little shrug. "Well, if I ever need a date, I just ask her."

For me, that arrangement was sufficient for the time being. It was all I could handle both socially and financially.

Following high school, I entered the junior college, so my hours in the classroom were reversed. Now I worked from 3:30 a.m. until noon, and attended classes in the afternoon. As my time with Gracie became more limited, I began to realize how I missed seeing her.

In spite of, or perhaps because of, these new restrictions, by the end of my college freshman year—at one of those famous parlor dates—I finally mustered up the courage to ask her to be my wife. I'll be forever grateful that Gracie said yes.

Since Adventists prefer not to wear jewelry, I presented her with a lovely Bible with a cover of Moroccan leather as an engagement gift. Then, in the fashion of the times, I wrote a letter to Gracie's mother back in Mississippi asking for Gracie's hand in marriage. We were engaged for a full year.

In the spring of 1940, it was Gracie's turn to graduate from high school. She then traveled back home to Mississippi to visit family members, whom she'd not seen for two years, returning to Tennessee in late June. Since I was scheduled to have the Fourth of July holiday off work—which fell on a Thursday that year—we set that as our wedding date.

Some friends of ours owned a large farm in Georgia. When this family learned of our upcoming marriage, they offered to let us hold the wedding in their ample farmhouse. I quickly lined up a retired minister to officiate, and commandeered our closest friends from school to stand up with us.

Although there were no flowers nor photos and only a few guests, we excitedly and joyfully exchanged our vows. My tiny, 98-pound bride wore a lacy, rose-colored dress, accented with a trim navy hat and matching pumps and handbag. Not too fancy by some standards, but to my eyes, she was the most beautiful bride in the world. In our hearts, our vows were exchanged as a commitment for a lifetime. That holiday weekend became our short honeymoon.

I'd just completed my second year of college, but since my draft number was so low the draft board convinced me it was futile to remain in school. They insisted that I'd be called up any day. As it happened, nearly three years passed before the draft caught up with me. But following their advice, I

★★

dropped my studies and became night foreman at the mill. Gracie worked there in the daytime.

We set up housekeeping in a small apartment that, at first, was only a rented room. Later the landlord added a bath and small kitchenette where we soon placed a dinette set and an electric range. It may have been tiny, but it was home sweet home.

During our years at Collegedale, observing the Sabbath had become a natural part of our lives together. From sundown on Friday until sundown on Saturday we did no work, but rather attended Sabbath school and church, filling the afternoons with activities that kept our hearts turned toward God. Our faith in a loving God grew along with our love for each other.

Life was very nearly perfect. Our savings grew, we made new purchases, and living was now a little more comfortable. Our very first car sat proudly in the driveway—a 1941 cream-colored Oldsmobile. Man, was I ever proud of that car!

Then came the infamous day that changed the lives of all Americans—December 7, 1941.

CHAPTER NINE

O ur nation was plunged into war, and it was clear that I'd soon be called up to go. Gracie and I made the very difficult decision to quit the hosiery mill and take the time to visit both our families. We stayed with Gracie's mother for a few weeks, then traveled on to Florida. In Tampa, we rented a small two-bedroom bungalow with a screened-in porch. It was a cozy little house that Gracie dearly loved.

For a time, I worked with my brother driving a truck route selling cookies. After learning the ropes, I found, to my great surprise, that I was a pretty fair salesman. Some of my best customers were the PXs and commissaries at nearby McDill Air Field.

During that hot summer of 1942, we learned we were going to have a baby. Our joy and excitement was mixed with the dread that any day I might be called up. Nearly all the young men in the nation were going off to the war, and Gracie and I knew we were living on borrowed time.

Paul Harold, Jr., made his appearance on St. Patrick's Day that next spring. Arrangements had been made for Gracie to go to St. Joseph's Hospital to have the baby. But when I borrowed the neighbor's phone that morning to call the hospital, I learned, to my dismay, there were expectant mothers waiting in its hallways. The war had created an

amazing number of shortages—doctors and medical personnel being one of them.

I phoned Gracie's doctor and he instructed us to go to
Tampa General. We did as he said, but it was almost as
crowded there. Nineteen babies were born that night at
Tampa General. All were girls, except for little Paul. The babies were brought to the mothers at scheduled times, and
Gracie told me she could always tell when our son was crying. The lusty cry of the Pervis boy coming down the hallway was much stronger and deeper than that of the baby
girls. It became the joke of the ward that Gracie quickly recognized the cry of Paul, Jr.

I never remember being as proud as I was when I looked
into the face of that tiny innocent baby. I could scarcely believe I was a father. We brought little Paul home to our bungalow on Louisiana Avenue.

During this time I'd hoped to get a job at the shipyard,
but that never materialized. So when the baby was 6 weeks
old, we decided to move to Palma Sola, just across the river
from Sneads Island where Dad lived.

By this time Dad had married a young woman named
Gladys Van Doren. Since Dad needed help on the farm, it
just seemed the right time for me to quit the cookie route
and return to farming.

The venture, however, was short-lived. By that next fall
my number finally came up and I received my long-awaited
notice from Uncle Sam.

I was registered as 1-A-O, which designated me as a
"conscientious cooperator." This term demonstrated my will-
ingness to serve in the military, while choosing not to take
up arms. Most SDA servicemen went into the military as
CO's, willing to cooperate as long as they were not asked to

violate their first allegiance to God and His commands.

There were, of course, some conscientious objectors who chose not to wear a uniform or salute the flag. These men were sent to camps around the country, where they worked until the war was over. As a rule, Seventh-day Adventists were not among them.

It was only a few days before Christmas, 1943, when I left for induction at Camp Blanding, Florida. There, as in hundreds of other induction centers all across the nation, scores of young men were herded through physical exams like so many cattle through the loading chute: X-rays, dental checks, blood pressure, inoculations.

That night, trying to sleep in the open bay, I wondered if every man being inducted suffered with a bad cold. Coughing echoed through the place like a kennel of barking dogs. The noise and the strangeness of the place prevented sleep. I simply wasn't accustomed to being away from home.

After passing the Army physical, I was told that their quota was filled for the time being. I was then given a choice of going into the Navy or the Marines. Since I'd been informed that the Navy was more lenient with Seventh-day Adventists and our desire to observe Sabbath worship, I chose the Navy.

The next day I was sent by train to Jacksonville, Florida, to be sworn in by the Navy. A number of other inductees were with me. It was too late in the evening to be processed when we arrived, so the Navy put us up for the night. I was taken to a rooming house, where I was given a room with a bed fitted with a thick feather mattress. What a difference from the previous night. Dog-tired from the travel and the emotional turmoil, I could hardly wait to crawl in that soft bed. But after only a few minutes' sleep, I was awakened by the painful bites of bedbugs. There was little sleep that night either.

The Navy gave me yet another physical, which took the entire day, and by now it was Christmas Eve.

After finally being sworn in, I was desperate to get to the train station and get a ticket back to Bradenton for Christmas. There was an endless wait to board the train, then I traveled all night, attempting fitful catnaps on the lurching train.

At 8:00 the next morning I was met at the station by Gracie and Paul, Jr. Thoroughly exhausted, I was still unspeakably happy to be back with my little family once again.

We spent Christmas at my grandparents' home. Many of my relatives had never met my Gracie, and I enjoyed showing her off. It was a warm day, and we spent it outdoors enjoying the Florida sunshine and each other.

The strain of the next few days was almost unbearable as I set about finding suitable and affordable housing for Gracie and the baby. Even though it tore our hearts out, we sold most all our nice furniture and Gracie moved in with a widow who had two young sons.

Soon the affairs were settled, and it was time for me to leave again. Gracie was now on her own to deal with the home and family matters. Her allotment from the Navy would be a mere $85.00 per month—a great deal less than what she'd been accustomed to the past few years. Making ends meet was not going to be easy.

I reported back to the Naval Base in Jacksonville and soon boarded a rickety old train bound for Chicago. From there I traveled farther north to Waukegan, Illinois—a long way from my sunny Florida home.

When I arrived at the base, I received my issued uniforms for work and dress, along with bedding and other necessary items. All new recruits were glad to settle down for the night after such a long trip, but my rest was not to be. For some reason, known only to the Navy, I was given the duty of taking care of other new arrivals throughout the night—issuing bedding and assigning them places to sleep. An interesting initiation into the Navy.

Here, during basic training, I learned the Navy way of doing things. No clothing or gear, other than that which was issued, was allowed. Everything I had fit neatly into the seabag and ditty bag. While I was in camp, my mattress was placed on top of the hammock, but when traveling, it was lashed around my seabag. Quite a handy little plan.

Each day was filled with training, exercises, marching, and of course, hard work. Scrubbing the wooden floors of the barracks was a routine chore. Ingenious sailors simplified this by placing steel wool beneath their shoes and scooting back and forth. This was aptly named "The Great Lakes Shuffle."

I had no problems at all with Sabbath worship during the three months of basic training. In fact, I met several other Navy recruits who were Adventists and we attended church together in Waukegan.

During the war, any and all troop movements were kept top secret. So when my group was prepared to transfer out after boot camp, we were given orders to report to a certain drill hall. We sat and waited through the afternoon until nightfall before boarding the troop trains. The long ride lasted through the night and into the next day. We were heading west, but that was about all we knew. The view out the windows was one of great expanses of open prairies. Eventually, we went through the mountains, but then came the hot desert.

The windows had to be kept open to allow air in, but with it came a film of powder-fine dust that coated everything. Pulling down the window shades helped a little, but not much.

After five days it was clear we were destined for California. Along the way, we were often sidetracked to wait for civilian passenger trains to pass. Finally, our train pulled in to San Diego, California. From that point, some of my buddies were sent to ships destined for who knew where. Others were sent to various stations or bases around the country.

I, however, was assigned to a training school for hospital corpsmen. The war in the Pacific was escalating and the number of casualties had increased the demand for more medics. The study course, therefore, was accelerated. During my years at Southern, I had learned how to pack plenty of studying into short pockets of time. Now that training paid off.

When our schooling was nearly complete, it was announced to our class that we were being assigned to the Marines. At that time the Navy was furnishing one medic for every six Marines. The Navy medics were even hitting the beachheads with the Marines. We were further told that the Japanese were shooting medics first in battle. Because of that, the Navy now required medics to carry side arms, and to learn how to use them. But when it came time to go to the firing range, I was exempted from bearing arms because of my 1-A-O classification.

One question that constantly concerned me was whether problems might arise with regard to my religious beliefs. I'd been told by other Adventists that problems occurred from time to time. That was when I decided to carry Circular 115-43 in my pocket. This notice to all ships and stations outlined the Navy policy with regard to observance of the Sabbath on days other than Sunday. The circular stated:

> . . . *when military circumstances permit, to excuse from duty*
> *on any week day, or part thereof, Naval personnel who desire to*
> *attend religious services, or to observe the Sabbath . . . provided*
> *such personnel are available for duty on Sunday in lieu of such*
> *week day.*

The piece of paper became yellowed and dog-eared, but I made certain I never went anywhere without it.

All during corps school we had weekends off, so I and a few friends attended church in San Diego. Following the completion of my schooling, my assignment was working on a ward caring for the sick. I was given every other weekend off.

Once the work routine was established and I had a measure of spare time, I thought more and more about Gracie and little Paul. It looked as though I might be staying in San Diego for a time, so I encouraged Gracie to bring the baby and come to California to be with me for whatever time we might have. But it was easier to lay the plan than to accomplish the feat, especially with the severe rationing that existed during wartime.

Shortly after I left for boot camp Gracie's mother became ill, so Gracie moved back home to Vicksburg, Mississippi, to care for her mother. Gracie and her sister both worked while her mother tended to Paul, Jr., and in this way they were able to make ends meet.

Even though Gracie had driven our Oldsmobile to Vicksburg, for the most part it sat idle. Gas ration stamps were scarce, and walking or taking the bus was the order of the day. Later, she wrote me that she was able to get a job at a hosiery mill that paid a little more than the local five-and-dime store.

When it came time for Gracie and Paul to come out to

California, my industrious young wife purchased a small house trailer. She then located another family who wanted to go to California as well. This couple had a toddler about Paul's age. Together the two families made the trek from Mississippi to San Diego, sharing the expenses and the driving.

As they crossed the heat of the desert, they drove only at night, making certain the gas tank was full. Water was nearly as scarce as the gasoline, and water was vital when traveling with two little ones. Most gas stations gave a quart of water along with a purchase of gasoline. Gracie remembers that she and the couple would take only small sips and give the rest to the toddlers. It was a long, tedious trip, and of course I was extremely concerned about their safety.

When they arrived at the California border, Gracie put through a long-distance call to me. When I got on the line, however, there wasn't much talking. Gracie was so grateful to hear my voice, and so eager to be with me that she couldn't stop crying. And I felt the same way. It was a happy moment when I was once again reunited with my wife and son and held them tightly in my arms.

As it turned out, we had only a few short weeks together in San Diego before orders came to report to Norfolk, Virginia. But they were days filled with the joy of simply being together. Now it was time to make another trek back across the continent. We attempted to sell our little trailer but were unable to do so, and wound up leaving it with an acquaintance. He promised to try to sell it for us, but we never heard from him again. In times of war, nothing is sure.

My SDA buddy, James Riggs, was shipped to Virginia before I was, and he wanted to know if his wife, Mildred, could travel back with us. Of course, in days of rationing, the more the better, so our answer was yes. The more people, the more books of ration stamps there were to share!

This return trip was far easier on Gracie, since I was there to help her, and there was no trailer to worry about towing. But at the end of this journey we would once again be parting—to who knew what fate.

Upon arriving in Virginia, we checked in at a little motel cabin. Places to stay were extremely hard to find during those times, especially any area near a military installation. I had only a few days before having to report to the base. Once I reported, I never was given another leave, even though I was there for several more weeks.

Gracie stayed nearby until she knew my ship had departed, then she left to go back home to Mississippi to continue her long wait. In my opinion, she was just about the best wife a guy could have. And to think I was causing a hardship on her because of the misunderstanding with the officers at the base. Somehow I felt she deserved better, but I also knew she would stick by me no matter what.

CHAPTER TEN

Back in Mississippi, when Gracie received word from James Riggs that her husband and five friends were in military prison because they refused to work on the Sabbath she quickly set to work. Riggs had sent her the names of the other men and their next of kin, so she wrote to Elder Carlyle B. Haynes, general secretary of the Seventh-day Adventist War Service Commission in Washington, D.C. As clearly as she could, Gracie explained to Elder Haynes what had happened, then informed him she would write to the family members of the other five.

Writing to the other families, young Gracie encouraged them to place calls or write letters to their local church groups, as well as their congressmen and senators. She told them that she planned to do the same. Much of her money—of which there was precious little—went for postage, and she spent many hours writing letters.

It was interesting to note that no two of our little group of prisoners were from the same state. Our hometowns were scattered from California to Pennsylvania to Florida and points between. Thus, the incident affected a large sector of American citizenship.

As early as October 8, W. E. Read, president of the Caribbean Union Conference, sent a letter to Elder Haynes explaining more of the details:

Elder C. J. Ritchie, the President of the South Caribbean Conference and I went over to the base and we were fortunate in interviewing the captain, who is the one in absolute charge of that particular section. We saw him together with the Legal Advisor of the camp and really had quite a round with them. We talked about the special provision made for our men, but we came away with the impression that these two men knew very little of our work, of our beliefs or of our position . . .

After we had discussed the matter, however, it was very evident that both men were able to see our position and that these boys might have disobeyed from conscience sake, and not from any disposition to be disobedient to orders.

He went on to brief Elder Haynes on the proceedings of the court-martial. Concerning that trial, he gave this hopeful bit of insight:

All the evidence was brought in and it appears that the court took a very charitable, favorable view of the whole situation, and it looks now as though when the decision is rendered, that there might be some little monetary fine imposed. Now this, of course, is anticipating things, but everything points in that direction at the moment.

The man to whom this letter was addressed, Elder Carlyle B. Haynes, was highly respected in areas of both business and government. Having served as an SDA pastor since the age of 23, he was, at the time of our trial, 62 years old. His appointment to the War Service Commission came in 1940, a post he had also held during the First World War. This wouldn't be the first time Elder Haynes had gone to bat for the people of his denomination, and his dogged determination would become a blessing to the six of us SDA boys.

Back in the Navy brig in Trinidad sat six young men who would have been forever thankful if Pastor Read had been correct in his speculation of the sentence. A "little monetary fine" would have been easy punishment. But it was not to be.

The days dragged by as we waited to be "read off," as it was referred to in Navy terms—to receive the verdict from the trial. If time had seemed endless prior to the trial, now the tension and apprehension were multiplied many times over. Up to this point, the orders remained the same—we were confined to our bunks day after day. The most difficult part of our punishment, however, was the withholding of our mail. Sailors away from home lived for mail call, and this lack of news from home created an enormous void in our lives.

It was to be a two-week wait before the verdict came down. On October 16, 1944, we heard the sounds of approaching footsteps. Within minutes a uniformed figure entered—the young lieutenant who had questioned me when I was in solitary confinement. We were called out to the desk on the double. As we stood at attention before him, he unfolded the papers and began to read, beginning with all our names. Then he continued: ". . . were tried by general court-martial by order of the Commander, Naval Operating Base, on 2 October 1944 and found guilty of the charge of Disobeying The Lawful Order of Their Superior Officer.

"Each of you," he went on without taking a breath, "is to be reduced in rating to apprentice seaman. You are to serve 24 months at hard labor at Portsmouth Naval Prison, Portsmouth, New Hampshire, then to be discharged from the U.S. Naval Service with a dishonorable discharge."

I watched as the officer abruptly turned and marched out just as quickly as he had come. We were speechless. Stunned beyond belief. The major had said he would ask for the stiffest sentence possible short of the firing squad, and he was true to his threat.

Prison. The very word sent chills through me in spite of the heavy tropical heat of the afternoon.

If we were shocked, I believe the turnkeys were even more shocked. It had become blatantly apparent to everyone there that we were not troublemakers. Perhaps they were beginning to think we'd gotten the raw end of the deal. At any rate, from that moment on our treatment changed. We were still not allowed to talk, but we could move about the cages and engage in much-needed, though still inadequate, exercise.

At this point, all we knew was that we were waiting for transport to return us to Stateside to begin our prison term. How long that wait would last, no one knew. Or at least, no one was telling us.

True to his sanguine nature, Pitrone got the bright idea to ask for a dictionary. He knew that in the back of the dictionary was the sign language alphabet. He set about learning it, and then taught it to all of us. This brilliant bit of thinking proved to be a delightful distraction. With slight body turns, we could cover up our signaling, and since this was our only means of conversing, we became adept quickly. The new opportunity for conversation was as refreshing to us as our new freedom of movement.

One day we had a new type of visitor, a curious little monkey. He came skittering and chattering down around the outside of the brig enclosure. Because of his fun-loving actions, we guessed he was a pet of one of the sailors on the base. His show gave us a good laugh. But later that evening, the irony of it struck me—here I was behind bars and the monkey was looking in at *me*. Not too funny!

As we waited out the long days, letters were zinging back

Sneads Island home, where Harold was born (bottom left window), Palmetto, Florida; 1917

Maud Lenora Craig Pervis, Harold's mother; circa 1909

George Barton Pervis, Harold's father; circa 1909

The Pervis boys (left to right): Harold, Arthur, Laurence, Irvin, Emory; circa 1920

Harold and Gracie Beaube on her graduation day from Collegedale Academy, Collegedale, Tennessee; 1940

Harold and Gracie after their wedding; 1940

Four generations of Pervis men (left to right): Jonas, George Barton, and Harold holding son, Paul H. Pervis, Jr.; 1943

"The Castle"—U.S. Navy prison,
Portsmouth, New Hampshire; circa 1943

Portrait of Harold; 1945

Harold's favorite picture of Gracie and
Paul, Jr., while he was overseas; 1945

Harold (center rear) with friends; Aleutian Islands, Adak, Alaska; 1945

Vesterlide Alden; 1945

Russell Pitrone; Aleutian Islands,
Adak, Alaska; 1945

Top: Aerial view of
Adak, Alaska; 1944

Center: Quonset
hut; Aleutian
Islands, Adak,
Alaska; 1945

Left: W. Duane
Montgomery; 1945

Right: Harold in
living quarters;
Aleutian Islands,
Adak, Alaska; 1945

Four of our group sent to Hawaii (left to right): Buckley, Alden, Boundey, Montgomery; Hawaii; 194

Harold by jeep; Aleutian Islands,
Adak, Alaska; 1945

Gracie and Harold (rear) with Dorinda and Paul,
Madison College, Tennessee; 1948

Harold with Russell Pitrone; Roundup, Montana; 1992

Vesterlide Alden; later years

Harold and Harry Buckley; Minneapolis, Minnesota; 1992

Harold, Gracie, Dorinda, and Paul; at fiftieth wedding anniversary; Palmetto, Florida; 1990

Harold being presented with plaque by Chaplain Major
Harold S. Johnson, Civil Air Patrol, on behalf of the
Southern College of SDA Alumni; Collegedale,
Tennessee; 1993

Above: Plaque inscription honoring Harold; Collegedale,
Tennessee; 1993

Left: Harold, Dorinda, The
Honorable Desmond T. Doss
(Congressional Medal of Honor,
honoree, and Dorinda's uncle by
marriage) at awards dinner;
Collegedale, Tennessee; 1993

Harold and Gracie's
house today (Harold
sleeps in same room
where he was born,
bottom left window);
Sneads Island,
Palmetto, Florida;
1997

and forth from Port of Spain to Washington, D.C. On October 19, W. E. Read wrote this to Elder Haynes:

> . . . with all the courtesies that have been extended to us as visitors and the kindly remarks and everything made by those in authority, you can see [from the trial transcript] the result of the trial is anything but satisfactory. The sentence is based particularly on one fact and that is disobedience to orders, and there is no indication at all that such disobedience was a matter of conscience. All that came out at the trial but in reading the result one would never gather that the difficulty was a religious one.
>
> Just at this point of this letter, might I mention that Elder Ritchie has just come into my office from a visit to the Base. He had an interview today with the authorities there and it seems quite evident that they have given the maximum penalty for an Advanced Base, and they have done this with the thought in mind particularly of making it a test case so as to arrest the attention of those higher up.

Elder Read went on to explain to Haynes that three of us had families who were dependent upon our Navy allowances—namely Alden, Buckley, and me. He suggested that the General Conference take steps to meet the need.

Just six days after our trial, on October 8, the commandant of the Tenth Naval District (which included Trinidad), Vice Admiral Giffen, issued his own order regarding treatment of those who observe the seventh-day Sabbath. Under "subject" it stated: "Seventh-day Adventists, policy in regard to employment on Saturday."

The order stated:

> Bona fide members of the 7th-day Adventist faith, provided there are no military reasons to the contrary, may be relieved of

all except routine duties from midnight Friday until midnight Saturday for the purpose of devoting this time to religious worship. Individuals so excused will be considered first on the list for police or any other duty found to be necessary on Sunday.
Robert C. Giffen

The fact that this order had no effect whatsoever on our trial or our sentence seemed to prove that Elder Read was correct in his assumption that they were attempting to make ours a test case.

Elder Haynes had his work cut out for him. His strategy, once he was clear on the surrounding circumstances, was twofold. Elder Haynes wanted first to get our court-martial sentences thrown out, or at least mitigated, and second, to force the Navy once and for all to clarify its position regarding Seventh-day Adventist beliefs with a satisfactory blanket order. An order that would clearly define a Navy commander's course of action should he find himself confronted with those of our faith who refused to perform unnecessary duties on Saturday.

Our mail privilege was now restored, and I excitedly wrote letters to Gracie trying to explain everything that had happened.

The letters from Elder Read caught up with Haynes in a hotel room in Cleveland, where he was attending the SDA Autumn Council meeting. From there on October 26, Haynes wrote to assure Read and Ritchie that he was on top of the situation:

> *. . . I am writing to tell you that I have submitted all of these cases to Secretary of the Navy and asking for a review of each case and for leniency to be exercised in their settlement.*

Haynes closed this letter by asking about our physical condition, since he'd heard we were being starved to the point of emaciation and weakness.

Of course, we were not in as bad shape as Elder Haynes had heard, but we certainly shed a good many pounds during our days of confinement. The worry and stress alone served to wear us down, and there were no trips to the canteen for ice cream or candy.

Ritchie wrote back to Haynes giving more of his view of what had transpired. His letter of October 30 stated:

> *Talking with the presiding judge, it seems to me that he understood what was involved. This is why I was so surprised at the severity of the sentence. I tried to point out to him that when the Navy Sabbath ruling, circular 115-45, is placed beside the General Navy (Sabbath) Sunday order that it was very clear what should be the privileges allowed Seventh-day Adventists, but like others of the officers he claimed that that was a matter of difference of opinion. In other words, Brother Haynes, I am driving at this point, the legality of the order which caused the boys to be sentenced should be questioned. In the open trial that feature was not discussed.*

Elder Ritchie went on to state that he wished the executive officer at the hospital would be replaced, since all the trouble began with his "unsympathetic and somewhat narrow attitude." Ritchie also explained that there had been no shortage of workers for the outside work in question that day:

> *As a matter of fact, there was difficulty at the time to know what to do with some of the men. This should enter into the decision of the higher courts, in view of the fact that this point is embodied in the Navy Sabbath order. A military emergency did not require the work, at that time, in any case.*

In closing, Ritchie assured Haynes that the large congregation at the Port of Spain church had been praying about the matter, "and we are expecting to see God work in wonderful ways."

Before the month of October was out, Elder Haynes wrote to Gracie to ask about the location of my voting residence, and indicated he planned to talk to my congressman about the situation. His letter of caring and concern did much to comfort Gracie. He said:

> I . . . will leave nothing undone to take care of the interests of these men.

As we soon learned, truer words were never spoken.

Yet one more letter was sent from the Port of Spain church, this one from Elder R. E. Cash addressed to Vice Admiral Giffen, commander of the Tenth Naval District. Cash minced no words as he appealed to Giffen's fairmindedness, especially in light of Giffen's order regarding Sabbath observance.

Cash briefly explained our situation in Trinidad, then added regarding the order:

> Some of the personnel here interpret that Order in such a way that they are privileged to either carry it out or ignore it, if they wish. Thus, it becomes quite easy for a doctor in charge of a Medical unit to make it difficult or easy for the men who come within the scope of that Order.

But Cash had even more ammunition in his diplomatic arsenal:

> I recently made representation to one of the British authorities in charge who gave this concession to Seventh-day Adventists

under his direction. Therefore, it seems strange to many here on the island that the local interpretation of American justice is not as broad as that of the local British military leadership. That, of course, makes it embarrassing for me as an American citizen.

Trusting that I may hear from you at your convenience and believing that you will do your very best in this case, I am, very sincerely yours, R.E. Cash.

The squeeze was on, and we six young sailors had become a very hot potato for the entire Navy! Of course, we didn't learn much of this for many long months. In some instances, it was years.

CHAPTER ELEVEN

B ecause the brig was set on a hill above the base we could see the harbor, and we squinted that direction many times a day, watching for the ship that would take us away. While I didn't relish going to prison, it seemed anything would be better than the day-upon-endless-day of waiting.

On Thursday evening, November 2, we finally saw it—the U.S.S. *Antaeus* making its way slowly through the quiet harbor waters. Our original sentence of a five-day stint in the brig had grown to 42 days. We were more than a little stir-crazy, and quite eager to be released, even if it would be for a short time.

Soon after the other prisoners were taken out to work the next morning, we were issued all the gear that had been taken away from us. I was shocked when I attempted to heave my seabag to my shoulder. I'd grown pitifully weak in just over a month of idleness. How would we be able to sling these bags around as we were transported?

Everything was finished. We were ready to depart, but of course, the transport truck didn't arrive until afternoon. It was the usual "hurry up and wait" for which the Navy was famous. When the truck finally arrived, we were surprised to note that the turnkeys and the chasers had gone soft on us. Their words of encouragement and genuine sadness at seeing us go did much to lighten our hearts. They knew we'd done nothing to deserve this stiff sentence.

With a great deal of effort, six very weak sailors threw their bags into the back of the truck and climbed in after them. After only a brief ride, we arrived at the dock beside the giant hulk of the *Antaeus*, right where we'd been only a few weeks prior.

A Navy guard yelled at us to line up near the foot of the gangplank. He shouted out our names and each of us raced up the gangplank into the smelly interior of the ship. There'd be no hours spent topside breathing in the fresh salt air on this trip. Not for the prisoners.

Once we were aboard, armed members of the ship's crew directed us down ladders, through passageways and hatches until we were deep within the bowels of the old ship. The air was foul even though ventilators were humming. We had no idea what was awaiting us. And the Sabbath was only a few hours away.

Our last final descent took us down a winding ladder where we landed on the steel deck plates of an enclosure situated just below the water line on the ship's port side. This was our "home" for the duration of the trip to New York Harbor. We wouldn't be gazing out into the soft green of the jungle. We couldn't hear the cheerful sounds of songbirds or the chattering of monkeys playing in the trees. There'd be no scent of the afternoon tropical rains. Just the rumble of deep innards of a seagoing vessel.

It crossed my mind that if something happened to the ship on the voyage, we'd be the last men out. Quickly I set that thought aside and tried not to allow it to come back to plague me. I remembered the Bible promise that my angel, which the Lord had assigned to me, would work miracles if it became necessary.

★★

Two other prisoners were already waiting in the brig, and we would pick up two more at Guantánamo Bay, Cuba. After the steel mesh door slammed and locked behind us, there was nothing left to do but find bunks and get ourselves squared away.

I wanted with all my heart to be on deck when the big old ship began steaming slowly out of that picturesque Trinidad harbor. Our being under lock and key made that impossible. Late that afternoon two sailors appeared at the mesh gate. Each had a pistol in a leather holster at his belt. While their side arms appeared ominous, their attitude was casual and friendly.

"You fellows get lined up and we'll take you up to early chow," one of them told us. This softer attitude was certainly a welcome change. My weakened legs were screaming at me as we crawled back up the winding stairs and ladders, and through the long passageways to the galley. This time, I didn't seem to mind the stench of garbage still pervading the kitchen area. At its worst, it was better than the stale air deep down in that brig. Chow time became a welcome break as we were let out for short periods of time to eat our meals.

Thankfully there was no more sitting with arms folded at attention before and after eating. In fact, I didn't even mind standing to eat after suffering under the strictly enforced rules back at the Navy base brig.

We were able to talk freely among ourselves as we ate, and our main topic of conversation those first few hours was the upcoming Sabbath. "From the looks of things," said Pitrone, referring to the lax guards, "this may be the most worry-free Sabbath we've had for a long time."

"Let's make it a noisy one," Buckley added. "How about a rousing Friday night song service?"

We agreed wholeheartedly.

After returning to the brig, we came to know our cell mates a little better. One was going to Portsmouth, as we were, destined to serve a life sentence for killing a man. The other was to spend a year at New York's Harts Island prison for drinking while on shore patrol duty.

When they asked about the six of us, we shared our story. They were shocked to hear that we were being punished for requesting to observe our religious freedom. We found this reaction to be typical whenever we recounted the episode.

As the time of sundown approached, we invited our new friends to join us in our Sabbath school service. We were pleasantly surprised that they seemed to enjoy themselves immensely as we sang, prayed, and read Bible scriptures.

That night I felt somewhat akin to Paul and Silas in the book of Acts (chapter 16). They had been thrown into prison, their hands and feet placed in stocks. Their only crime, their desire to serve their Lord. But even though they had been beaten, the two began to sing heartfelt praises to God, their music echoing throughout the corridors of the dark, dank prison. As a result the jailer and his entire household were brought to a saving knowledge of the Lord.

My feet were not in stocks, and my back wasn't bloody from a beating, but it was quite evident that our "jailhouse" praise service had a marvelous effect upon these two prisoners.

At the same time we were sailing through the dangerous waters of the Atlantic on our way to New York, the first response from a congressman landed on the desk of Carlyle B. Haynes in Washington, D.C. Now the name of the United States president himself was brought into the picture. J. Hardin Peterson, representative from the First District of Florida, wrote:

Thank you very much for your letter of the 10th regarding the above named constituent [referring to me.] I appreciate your bringing this case to my attention and I am anxious to be of all possible assistance. I am immediately taking the matter up with Secretary Forrestal [Secretary of the Navy under Roosevelt] and with the President. I shall be glad to advise you as the matter progresses. With all good wishes, I am sincerely yours, J. Harden Peterson

Our journey back to the States took an entire week. As the ship moved farther and farther northward, the temperature inside the brig dropped steadily. By the time the next Friday arrived, it was mighty cold and we six men, our bodies accustomed to the tropical air, were shivering. We dug in our bags for our warm blue uniforms and heavy pea jackets. However, when Pitrone went to get his coat it had mysteriously disappeared. He kept a good humor about it. I wasn't sure I would have been so forgiving.

Early Friday morning we heard sounds rumbling through the ship that we recognized as preparation for docking. Suddenly silence and a few bangs told us we were tying up somewhere. The time was 0845. We were certainly thankful to be released from the belly of that huge ship, but none of us would deny that we were filled with apprehension. Our Sabbath began at sundown. What would we face next? Would there be more trouble?

Buckley expressed the feelings of all of us when he muttered, "Why does everything have to happen on the Sabbath?"

We sat and waited. Then we waited some more. One would think by now we would have become accustomed to waiting, but it never came easy. Finally, at 2000 (10:00) footsteps came ringing down the metal ladder steps. A friendly voice sounded out. "All right, men. Get your gear. Let's go."

With hoisted seabags we did our best to keep up with our guard as he led us through all the long passageways and up the narrow stairways. At last we came out near the top of a gangplank.

The frigid wind of New York hit us like a smart slap in the face. I felt sorry for Pitrone, who had no coat. We all offered to trade off lending him our coats, but he wouldn't hear of it.

Below, at the foot of the gangplank, waited a group of shore patrolmen. They were milling around a few patrol wagons that were idling and sending puffs of dull, gray steam into the cold morning air. All of a sudden I heard the sound of a band striking up a rousing Sousa march. At once the music had a twofold effect on me. Sousa marches are able to stir the patriotic blood of almost any living, breathing American—me included. And yet, the knowledge that this band was in no way playing to welcome our little group depressed me deeply. Other ships were docking, too, and the band was no doubt welcoming troops home from the war in Europe.

Meanwhile, we were led down the gangplank to the waiting paddy wagons. Before loading us, a guard ordered us to halt. We were each frisked just in case we were trying to slip by with concealed weapons. In a short time we were loaded and the paddy wagon lurched forward, crawling through the narrow streets of New York.

Not one of our group had ever been to New York. We had no idea where we were located, nor where we were headed. We were certainly craning to try to see out through the mesh-covered openings and catch a glimpse of this immense city. Presently, our vehicle was driven aboard an auto ferry and we were moving through the choppy waters toward Manhattan.

I believe it was Pitrone who saw her first. At any rate someone shouted, "There she is!" Now we all rubber-necked to get a glimpse of the gray-green lady holding her flame high for all to see. The famed Statue of Liberty stood proud and tall on her grassy island, welcoming all who needed and craved freedom and liberty. Again, we were struck by this ironic twist.

It brought to my mind the sight of our nation's flag hanging limply behind the row of officers in the makeshift Trinidad courtroom as we were court-martialed for attempting to exercise religious freedom. Where was the freedom that these symbols proclaimed?

Our ferry berthed, and the paddy wagon chugged along toward our unknown destination. It was obvious we were approaching the wharves of lower Manhattan. Eventually we pulled to a stop. We saw an old ship covered with dull rust and in dismal condition. This forlorn sight sobered each one of us. This was the infamous *Camden* docked at Pier 92, a prison complex about which we had heard from other more savvy prisoners. This ancient ship, captured from the Germans during the First World War, had become a brig and was noted for its unsavory conditions.

We were marched up to the main deck of the decrepit floating fortress. Even if this hulk had been kept up and repaired, it would have been uninviting. But in its neglected state it was almost unfathomable that anyone would be sentenced to stay aboard her for very long. Personally, I was praying that our stay would be extremely abbreviated.

We were led down to a large litter-strewn hold occupied by approximately 50 other prisoners. The tiers of bunks that nearly reached the overhead were equally as dilapidated as the rest of the ship. The conditions were deplorable. Even though the weather was cold, some of the men slept on the steel deck. This was because the beds were simply broken steel springs with no mattresses. I chose the springs and covered them and myself with one blanket.

We were given trays of food at chow time and ate wherever we could find a place to sit down. Some prisoners were evidently on bread and water only, and were desperate for any little crust that could be begged off someone. We couldn't help wanting to share our food with them. It was difficult for me to believe these were my fellow sailors. I couldn't imagine any crime that would be deserving of such cruel treatment.

I peered out of a porthole reinforced with crosses of rusty steel at the dirty harbor water. It was nearly 1700 (5:00), and an early winter darkness was beginning to settle over the city. Suddenly over the blaring loudspeaker came this announcement: "Now hear this! Now hear this! Will prisoners Montgomery and Buckley report to the master at arms' desk immediately?"

We stood transfixed as all the bad experiences of the past few months tumbled through our minds. Quickly, I shook the thoughts away. "Get going," I said to the two men. "We'll be here praying."

While they were gone, we set about getting squared away, all the while praying quietly for whatever fate awaited our buddies. Presently they returned to us—with smiles on their faces. Their expressions alone were priceless.

It seems the MA took them to talk to the lieutenant in charge. "I've been reviewing your papers," the lieutenant said to the two sailor/prisoners. "I'm very interested in hearing your story of what happened down in Trinidad."

★★★

Having been tricked once before by an officer, both Montgomery and Buckley were extremely cautious, but they recounted detail-by-detail the events leading up to the court-martial. After finishing the story, they braced for the officer's response. But he surprised them by saying, "I think this entire episode is a shame and an embarrassment to the Navy. I would term this as religious persecution. If you were going to be here any time at all," he continued, "I'd reopen this case and order a retrial and try to get you out of this."

"We almost cried," Buckley told us. "Aside from Elder Ritchie's, these are the first words of compassion we've heard since everything broke loose in September."

"That's not all," Montgomery said. "Then he assured us we would not be called on to do any work this evening or tomorrow."

"What'd you say then?" Pitrone asked.

Buckley grinned. "All we could think to say was 'thanks.'"

By now the curiosity of the other prisoners had been aroused, all of whom welcomed a little excitement in their lives. Questions began flying about as to why we were in, and what was all this talk about religious persecution. One more time we told our story, and one more time we had a Sabbath service in a prison cell, this time with an even larger congregation. God was certainly getting the glory for all that had happened.

CHAPTER TWELVE

R eveille sounded Sabbath morning at the unbelievable hour of 0400. A cold, still fog hung over the harbor, blanketing everything with bone-chilling dampness. The dots of yellow lights on the dock were crowned in fuzzy halos. We were fed an unappetizing early-morning chow and then made ready to leave. This time there was no endless waiting.

As we returned from chow the loudspeaker blared its announcement: "Now hear this. The following prisoners will ship into their dress blues, collect their gear, and prepare to debark." Each of our names was called out along with eight others who would accompany us along the way to New Hampshire. I would be eternally grateful to leave the dirty decks of the *Camden*, in spite of the kindness shown to us by the commanding officer.

After collecting our gear, we reported to the MA's station, where we were introduced to a brand-new concept: handcuffs. I was incredulous. What next?

It was now 0520 on a cold, damp November morning. Down the gangplank we went, our seabags slung over our shoulders, the other hand shackled to a fellow prisoner. Now that called for careful dexterity. The next trick was to get loaded in the waiting van.

Pitrone was nearly blue with cold, and was finally given

✯✯✯

a worn, but very welcome, pea coat from one of the guards. I was never sure where that coat came from, but was thankful Pitrone now had a little more protection against the frigid air. None of us were warm, even with coats on. I was not sorry to leave Pier 92.

As the van lumbered through the streets of Manhattan, we spied a number of familiar landmarks, such as the Empire State Building, and the Woolworth Building. Everyone we saw seemed half frozen as they scurried along, bundled up tightly against sharp winds. In the back of that van we, too, were pulling our heads down inside our pea coats.

When a massive building loomed through the fog right in front of us, one of our group recognized it as Grand Central Station. Had we not been shackled and headed for prison, I'm sure we would have been quite impressed. Who had not heard of this gigantic edifice? It was as much a part of the American scene as the Statue of Liberty. What we'd not considered, however, was the fact that in this teeming public terminal we'd be a spectacle—a sight to be gawked at.

The guards stepped down from the warm van cab and we heard the hoarse command, "Everybody out!" Now the tricky maneuvering was reversed—jumping down to the pavement without yanking those bracelets and spraining a wrist. My shackled hand was numb from the cold as well as from lack of circulation. As we hit the ground we were surrounded by armed guards who directed us to form two columns.

I'd always heard the expression "busy as Grand Central Station," and now I understood the full meaning. Reared on a farm in Florida, I'd never seen so many people rushing about in a frenzy of comings and goings.

As much as possible I tried not to look one way or the other, but just keep my eyes straight ahead. However, I couldn't help seeing the shocked looks as people realized what our little entourage was all about. The cuffs were impossible to hide, not to mention the fact that the six of us still had shaved heads. I'm sure we looked like a group of dangerous men, and a few of our number actually were hardened criminals.

As we entered the cavernous structure, we were literally swept along with the moving crowd. Unfortunately, one guard brought more attention to us as he shouted, "Gangway!" People were more than happy to move quickly and give us a wide berth.

Further into the station, the guards located a group of empty benches clustered together and told us to be seated, since we were early for our train. We were thankful to sit and rest from lugging our seabags one-handed, but now more and more people stared and gawked at us. The embarrassment and humiliation was agonizing.

Our wait was short-lived. Soon we were ordered onto our feet and led through the turnstiles back out into the biting cold toward a waiting train. The coal-burner puffed billows of black gritty smoke into the still, cold morning. Thankfully, our bags were placed on carts to be taken to the baggage car. Not having our bags meant one less worry.

One of our guards went into our train car ahead of us, routing out a number of civilian passengers. This left empty seats so we could sit together with the guards close by. They could take no chances. We boarded carefully, turning gingerly down the narrow aisle with cuffs pulling and tugging at our chafed wrists. As with the people in the station, faces around us registered fear, shock, and then at last, disgust. I'm sure they were thinking that here was a bunch of sailors who had disgraced the uniform and the name of their country.

After all the prisoners were settled in, one guard stationed himself at the front of the car, another at the rear. A third paced up and down the aisle. I'm sure it made the civilian passengers feel nervous and unsettled.

As the "All aboard!" sounded from outside the train, a few last-minute arrivals bounded into the car, took one look, sized up the situation, and made a hasty retreat. I couldn't blame them. If I'd been in their shoes, I might have done the same thing.

The train began with little jumps and lurches as it pulled out from the boarding tunnel into the gray light of a cloudy November day. Now the guards, who had become rather friendly with us, came and loosened our shackles—much to our relief. I rubbed and rubbed at my wrist, forcing circulation back into my hand and soothing the pain from the chafing.

I watched as sooty, grimy New York slum areas, interspersed with dingy factories and manufacturing centers, whipped by the windows. I wasn't sure if all the gray was from the cloudy, foggy day, or from the towering, smoldering smokestacks of the active mills and factories. Probably both.

Within a short hour the scenery changed from that of a crowded, sooty city to quaint little New England villages tucked back into tree-covered hills. Steep-pitched cottages clustered around tiny churches with tall white steeples. After a week inside the *Antaeus*, and an unforgettable night on the *Camden*, this was indeed a pleasant change. I settled back and rested as the picturesque scenes passed by one after the other. I found myself wishing I could follow one of those winding dirt roads back into the quiet stands of birch and maple trees, and just sit there, soaking up the peace.

At intervals, our train stopped at antiquated little stations where a few locals stepped off into the arms of waiting loved ones. Watching the scenes made each of us more homesick.

As we traveled yet farther northward the farms were surrounded by low, thick rock walls built strong and precise by New England farmers from decades past. At times we neared the coast and saw miniature fishing villages huddled in quiet coves. I watched angry whitecaps forming out in the Atlantic, and foamy pounding waves smacking against the rocky shoreline. I shivered as I thought of that raw wind sweeping in off the water. My blood was thin and I knew it. The few months I spent last winter in Illinois proved that.

Presently, the train began to slow and the clacking rhythm slackened. Civilian passengers stirred, standing, stretching, and then bundling into heavy overcoats.

"Boston! Boston, Massachusetts," came the conductor's clear cry as he moved along through the cars. "All out for Boston!"

When all the other passengers were off, the guard again secured our handcuffs and instructed us to rise. We worked our way down the narrow aisles, down the steps and onto the station platform. Nothing could have prepared me for the shock of the winter wind. It stung like a million tiny needles, and seemed to suck the air right out of my lungs. Around about the station lay pyramids of soot-covered snow, having been shoveled and stacked there from a previous snowstorm. I guess I should have been thankful we didn't arrive in a blinding blizzard.

We were marched to a baggage area, where our bags were retrieved, then we stood about stamping our feet, and hunching our heads as deeply into our coats as possible. Our free hands were plunged into our coat pockets, our manacled hands tucked under a jacket flap for as much protection from the wind as it could provide.

As usual, we had to wait awhile before a truck came flying

around the corner and slammed to a halt. As much as we could, we assisted each other in throwing the seabags into the back, then worked in tandem to hoist our bodies up over the chin-high tailgate.

The truck took us across the city of Boston from the large main railroad station to another smaller station. The ride may have been short, but it was bitterly cold. By the time the truck stopped at this smaller out-of-the-way station, I was sure I had frostbite. It was a long time before the feeling came back to my ears and fingers, and when it did they stung and burned.

After we'd clumsily climbed down from the truck, we were led up the street to a little café. Now things were definitely looking up. Real food! I'll never forget the rush of warm air filled with the scent of good food as we entered that café. After all we'd been through, and all we'd experienced recently, this was an unexpected, special treat. The guards added to our comfort, releasing the six of us from our shackles. The handcuffs of the other eight prisoners remained securely fastened.

Years later, the details of what I ordered at that cozy neighborhood café are lost to my memory, but I'll never forget how I savored each and every bite. None of us knew but what it might be two full years before we'd experience a café, good food, and relative freedom again.

Upon hearing our story, our guards insisted that we would never serve out our full terms. While their remarks were comforting, it still wasn't the same as an ordered release. We could take only one day at a time.

From the café, we returned to the station at around 1400 (2:00 p.m.) and boarded a vintage late-1800s train coach. It looked like something out of a history book. It was headed up by an old-time locomotive from bygone days. I'm sure the war had something to do with this antique being taken out of mothballs. While it was an interesting bit of history, it was also quite drafty. Soon the warmth of the café was only a fading memory, and we were chilled for the remainder of our journey northward. Thankfully, our handcuffs remained off for the rest of the trip.

By the time we crossed over into New Hampshire, the stark forests were thicker, and the villages fewer. Snow lay about in thick patches, a constant reminder of the early winter this far north. The rosy glow of a cloudy sunset gave a pink cast to the drifts of snow. As the day began to close, and we drew nearer to our destination, our apprehension mounted. No one talked much now, but we each sensed the tension in the chilled interior of the old coach. At last the conductor pushed into our car calling out "Portsmouth, New Hampshire, next stop. All out for Portsmouth!"

"Well, this is it," Alden whispered beside me.

"My mouth feels dry as cotton," I whispered back. He only nodded.

We jolted to a stop beside a tiny station that matched our train in antiquity. The high-pitched roof and tall windows made it look like a small church. As before, we had to wait until all other passengers left before we could disembark.

The guards led us inside the station, where the protesting floorboards creaked beneath our feet. We were ordered to sit down on the hard wooden benches. An old-fashioned potbellied stove in the corner gave off spitting and popping noises. It was a comforting sound, but little heat reached anywhere near where we sat. While we waited, a guard used the telephone there to notify the prison that we had arrived. Much too soon we heard a truck rumbling up to the station. In came a burly Marine who glanced quickly at our Navy guards and then at us. "We've come for the prisoners," he said sharply.

Ah yes, more Marines. Our memories were fresh with regard to Marine guards. "Let's go, prisoners!" the guard barked.

We followed him out to the truck where another Marine guard waited. These Marines were astonished to find the six of us without our handcuffs on. "Hey," one Marine spouted, "these prisoners are your responsibility until we get through that prison gate. Don't you know the penalty for having an escape?"

We had learned this interesting rule some time ago. If a guard lost a prisoner, he himself would be required to serve out the term. That made for some pretty serious guards.

"Don't worry about these men," our Navy guard replied, referring to the six of us. "They wouldn't run away if you told them to."

In response, the Marine merely shrugged. However, that statement of trust did much to bolster our spirits.

One more time we were loaded into the back of a truck. As the sun disappeared below the horizon, the bitter nighttime cold set in again. The truck careened around a few corners, then stopped at an entrance gate where we heard our guards talking with a guard on duty there. Presently we crossed an arched stone bridge and approached a towering structure that looked like a medieval castle. Pale lights shone from its barred windows. I wasn't aware that America had any castles, but I now knew they had at least one and I was destined to spend two long years inside it.

The prison was situated on a large island at the mouth of the Piscataqua River between Kittery, Maine, and Portsmouth. With the Atlantic Ocean on one side, and a river full of whirlpools and eddies on the other, no one had ever escaped from the place. "The Castle," as it was referred to, was the Navy's largest prison in the country.

The square center block of the building stood tall and high with a pitched roof rising even higher. At each corner were round turrets with battlements mounted atop each one. It looked as if it were right out of Camelot. Arched windows and scalloped facings at the roof finished out this castle theme. Wings extended from each side of the center, one longer than the other, also complete with turrets topped with battlements. It was an impressive sight indeed.

A seven-story addition had been built at the far end of the longer wing. No turrets here, it looked more like a modern office building or hospital. Scattered about the grounds were a multitude of long, low buildings and Quonset huts that appeared to house various workshops.

In the ensuing days we learned more about this monstrous facility. A prison first existed here at Portsmouth Navy Yard in the form of a prison ship, the U.S.S. *Southery*. The ship was used from 1902 until 1908, when construction began on The Castle. First the center block and longer wing were built, with the second wing and annex being added later.

We were quickly unloaded from the truck and led up high stone steps, through a massive wooden door and into a vast waiting area, complete with a shiny marble floor. A Marine officer met us there and questioned each of us as to our treatment on the trip up from New York—if there had been any problems. We answered that there had been none. The officer then asked the guards if there had been any trouble with the prisoners. The reply again was negative.

After the usual exchange and review of documents, our guards turned to leave. As they left, they gave the six of us friendly smiles and nods. Still fearful of what lay ahead, that brief moment was reassuring and heartwarming.

We were told to sit down on benches that lined the wall. We were then processed in one at a time—a lengthy procedure. By that time we were tired and hungry. Our day, which began at 4:00 a.m., had been a long one. But finally the processing was over and a guard appeared. "Follow me," he said, opening a heavy door opposite the one in which we entered.

We found ourselves inside a giant cellblock that ran the length of the wings. This cellblock stood as a steel island in the middle, separated from the side and end walls by wide passageways. It was composed of tiers, four high, and about 150 to 200 feet long. I could see that the upper tiers were reached by steel ladders at each end. All the walls were painted white—spotless and clean. The large windows let in plenty of light.

I shivered as the eyes of all those caged men riveted on us. This was worse than any prison movie I'd ever seen. Our hollow footsteps created strange echoes through the mausoleum-like room as the guard led us down the passageway. No one spoke. I wondered if our cells were already picked out for us. Would any of us be together?

After walking the entire length of the cellblock, the guard opened yet another door, and we followed him through it into the annex. The aromas here were somewhat reassuring. This was the prison galley, and we were about to be fed our supper. I was so hungry I could have eaten the plates. The food was served cafeteria-style, and we passed in front of the steam tables with our trays ready.

As was our custom, the six of us bowed our heads to offer thanksgiving before eating. When I looked up again, one of the guards was staring at us.

"How did you fellows happen to wind up in prison?" he wanted to know.

Briefly we explained the events that had brought us to Portsmouth. The guard then wanted to know the length of our sentence. "Two years," Boundey replied.

"Well, I can tell you one thing," the guard said. "You'll work in this place—Sabbath or no Sabbath!"

His words had a sobering effect.

From the galley we were taken over into the newer addition, where our prison-issue clothing was dispensed. We had to hand over our blues, our dungarees, and our summer whites. As I held the folded dull gray prison uniforms, an almost indescribable wave of depression washed over me. It was hard to move, hard to change into these colorless, drab clothes, and painful to look about me and see my close buddies dressed the same.

Incidentals, such as soap and toothpaste, were issued, but we were told that after this, we'd have to purchase these items out of our $3.00 monthly allotment. Now that would take a small miracle. Even in 1944, $3.00 would never stretch that far.

The guard ordered us to follow him once again. We assumed we'd be going back to that crypt of cells and placed in our respective cages. To our great relief, we were taken instead to what was referred to as the "tank" on the third floor of the annex. Of course, we were unaware that only those considered escape risks were placed in the cellblock.

The tank was a long room filled with row upon row of double bunks—several hundred bunks in all. Out the windows, I could see boats and ships in the nearby harbor. The guard selected an unoccupied section, assigned us our bunks, and ordered us to square away our gear. When he turned to go, we were left unattended, except for the other prisoners who stayed there. What a good feeling to have a relaxed gab session together before turning in.

"I feel sure that since our church leaders are aware of what's going on," Boundey was saying, "that they'll be fighting in our corner."

"But what can a little church group do when put up against the entire United States Navy?" Alden asked.

"I've heard of the good things that Haynes has done," Buckley put in. "I understand he really knows his way around Washington."

"No matter how you look at it," I said, "we disobeyed a lawful order. Several of them as a matter of fact."

"But who's to say the command was lawful?" Montgomery countered. "Is it lawful to require us to forfeit our religious convictions? That's what we're supposed to be fighting for!"

"Right now, the most important thing is what might happen if we refuse to work next Sabbath," Buckley said. "The thought of spending two years in solitary confinement for refusing to work doesn't really appeal to me."

"Me either," I said, shaking my head.

But on the other hand, each of us knew we would not work on the seventh day, the Sabbath. We'd come too far to give up our allegiance to God now.

Suddenly the blinking lights signaled time for lights out. The Sabbath of November 11, 1944, was over. For the present, there had been no further complications. The Lord had promised to take us a step at a time, and at that moment I was thankful I was with my five friends. As I lay down and tried to get comfortable, I felt extremely thankful that I wasn't trying to sleep next to a violent criminal in one of those tiered cages with the bars.

CHAPTER THIRTEEN

The next day, Sunday, was relatively quiet. We were back to the pattern of total boredom, which had become so familiar to us in the brig in Trinidad. The work detail would no doubt begin the following morning.

That afternoon we met with the master at arms to receive the list of prison regulations, and to be apprised of our duties and responsibilities. "At this prison, everyone works," the MA stated in a flat, even tone, "and they don't put up with no foolishness."

That seemed as good a moment as any for us to state our situation. Buckley spoke up, explaining our religious convictions, and asked if we might forgo working on Saturdays. The MA looked startled. "Around here Saturday is like any other workday," he said firmly. "The only day off is Sunday. Everyone takes off on Sunday except those assigned to special rotating details like garbage pickup and galley duty." He scanned his clipboard as though to make certain he'd covered everything. "Take my advice, mates. Since you're going to be working on Saturdays here, you just as well forget the religious stuff for the time being."

The ominous pronouncement hit each one of us with an uneasy blow. We spent much of that afternoon in prayer and Bible reading.

On that same Sunday, in Washington, D.C., Elder Haynes was busy with various bits of correspondence that directly affected us. Several letters were sent to our home churches. The one to L. C. Evans, the president of the Florida Conference of our church in Orlando, read:

> I think it would be a very helpful thing if you would have the members of the church in Representative Peterson's district flood him with letters asking him to intervene in behalf of this man [referring to me] and see that he is released from this sentence. This would include all the churches which may be in the counties which comprise Representative Peterson's Congressional district. . . . Will it be possible for you to have announcements made in these churches giving the facts of the case, the name of the individual, and encouraging these members to get these letters of protest in just as quickly as possible . . . ?
>
> It will also help if the members of all churches in Florida will flood the offices of Senator Charles O. Andrews and Senator Claude Pepper with letters of protest about this case. These do not have to be confined to the members of the churches in Representative Peterson's district, but can come from any church in Florida.

Elder Haynes had now kicked his battle plan into high gear!

✂ ✂ ✂

Monday morning's 0530 (5:30) reveille came much too early. The arctic chill of New England penetrated the prison walls and seeped up through the flooring. The blustery winds wailed around outside the windows, and I began to doubt I would ever feel warm again. We wondered if our work detail would take us out into the onslaught of that wicked wind.

★★

However, following breakfast, when the others left for work our small group remained behind. The situation was strangely reminiscent of the one in Trinidad. No one seemed to know how to make connections with the prison authorities so we could find out what was happening.

Later that day we were run through a battery of interrogations. We were never sure if the men who questioned us were lawyers or what, but they certainly knew their business. We were questioned in minute detail about our backgrounds. It was relentless. I felt as though I was suspected of having links with organized crime or some such terrible thing. Somehow this had an effect on our emotions as nothing had before. Even the handcuffs failed to affect us in the way this rigid interrogation had—we felt like full-fledged criminals.

Tuesday and Wednesday mornings we were once again left behind as the others went to work. Then shortly after the noon chow time, Wednesday, a guard came up and asked which of us was Pervis. I'm sure my expression registered surprise and shock. "That's me," I answered. The others were looking at me and wondering, *What now?* I was wondering, *Why me?*

"Come with me," was all the guard said. I followed him down a few hallways and into an office area. Presently, I was informed that the commander of the prison, Colonel J. A. Rossell, wanted to speak with me. Now this was quite a turn of events. I snapped to attention before him. "At ease," said the slender, graying officer. Then he motioned me to a nearby chair. I sat down but was quite uneasy.

"Why are you in prison?" was the colonel's first question. He seemed pleasant enough, but we'd been tricked before, so I answered as briefly and simply as possible. "I and my friends are here because of our religious beliefs, sir," I told him.

His brows raised as he nodded. "Oh yeah. You're one of the six that got canned down in Trinidad over your religion. Bunch of narrow-minded guys down there if you ask me."

Now I was even more surprised and didn't know how to reply. We'd held this thought in our minds since the very beginning, but to have another officer voice the same opinion was extremely reassuring.

The colonel straightened and leaned forward. "I'll guarantee you, sailor," he said looking right at me and tapping the desk with his pen for emphasis, "as long as you are here none of you will be required to work on the Sabbath. And furthermore, I'll see to it that you have a place designated for your worship area."

It was a good thing I was sitting down or I might have dropped to the floor in shock. That officer probably never knew what his words and his kind gesture meant to six young Seventh-day Adventists. The terrible gnawing fear that had been eating at each of us suddenly disappeared. I felt I could easily serve the two years in prison, just knowing that I wouldn't have to wrangle with anyone over observance of the Sabbath.

I could hardly wait to tell the others the good news, and what a time of rejoicing we had. We hardly realized the burden we'd been carrying, how it had colored our every thought. Knowing that week after week we wouldn't have to fight to worship, we could face anything now!

Before the week was out, we were given odd jobs to do. One of my jobs was having to carry a mattress cover filled with heavy boots from one building to another. What a struggle that was. Another day found me out in the cold pouring a concrete foundation for a new building.

Eventually, though, all six of us wound up out on the

infamous rock pile. The job of that particular work crew was to make little rocks out of big rocks using 16-pound sledge hammers. The prison had a contract with the state of New Hampshire for all the road-building gravel the prisoners could produce.

Now we learned just how weak our bodies had become during the weeks of enforced idleness. The smack of that hammer on solid granite sent shock waves clear up to our shoulders. None of us had enough strength for the job, and we were expected to keep at it without stopping. But we could pray as we worked, and we did. God helped us. We never doubted for a moment that we were working in His strength. He sustained us moment by moment, and hour by hour to endure this punishing pace.

The guard let us know right away that we were not to rest other than during the designated times. "If you want to rest any other time," he said, "hold your hammer over your head while you do it." Needless to say, no one felt the urge to rest much.

We broke rock in snow and icy rain, as well as when the sun shone. But at that time of year, there wasn't much sunshine. The relentless cold was a constant plague, chilling us deep in the bone.

Knowing how the lines of communication in the military can break down, I wondered that first week if everything was in place for us to have Saturday off. But before the time came, we were advised by the warden himself that we were to have Saturday free. "You men will be expected to make up your time on Sundays in a manner that is equitable with the other prisoners who are required to work on Saturdays." We all readily agreed. That was no problem for us.

We were given access to the prison auditorium to use for

our Sabbath afternoon service. It was large, well-built, and nicely furnished with a stage and comfortable theater-style seats. Quite a surprise to see this in a prison. Using a few of the front seats, we gathered around and conducted a service that cheered our hearts. We praised God for this miracle of an understanding and sympathetic commander.

The afternoon of our first Sabbath, we were in the tank enjoying fellowship with one another when the quiet was interrupted by the crackling of the loudspeaker. "Will the following men ship into your dress grays and report to the MA's office immediately? You have a visitor." Then each of our names was called out.

We were incredulous. A visitor? For us? But we wasted no time in getting changed and reporting. From the MA's office we were led up several flights of stairs—the prisoners were never allowed to use the elevator—to the auditorium. We had just stepped into the auditorium when the elevator opened. Out stepped a well-dressed stranger escorted by a guard. I immediately thought he looked like an Adventist preacher. He came toward us with an outstretched hand and a wide smile.

"I'm Pastor Aldridge of the local Seventh-day Adventist church in Rochester, New Hampshire," he said. "I've come to see how you boys are doing."

We could hardly believe our good fortune.

"We've heard about you," he added, shaking hands with each one of us, "and I've come to inquire about your welfare."

It was an exhilarating experience to sit down and visit with yet another SDA pastor, a man truly concerned about what had happened to us. We poured out our story to him. In return, he told us what he knew of the work on our behalf in Washington, D.C.

He told about the flood of letters of protest piling up on the desks of congressmen and senators. "However, I must warn you," Pastor Aldridge added, "that it will take time. The Navy moves at a snail's pace in these types of situations."

Somehow, for the moment none of that seemed to matter. We were overjoyed that someone in this cold, desolate, out-of-the-way spot knew we were there, and genuinely cared about us. I felt a prickling behind my eyes, and blinked so I wouldn't cry.

Pastor Aldridge also reminded us what a fighter Elder Haynes could be. "He doesn't easily take no for an answer," he said. "He won't give up or quit. But you may have to be patient for a time."

After we'd visited for nearly an hour the pastor rose to leave. "It was a pleasure to spend time with you," he said, "and I'll be back as often as they will allow. Pastor Ochs, president of the New England Conference, wants to try to get over to see you as well." And with that good word, and a prayer for our safety, he left.

It was with great joy and thanksgiving that we threw ourselves into the work of collecting garbage the next day. The work was easier because in our hearts we knew that we'd not been forgotten.

By the middle of November, Elder Haynes was beginning to see some response from the legislative branch of the government. An encouraging letter arrived on his desk from Representative J. Hardin Peterson:

> For your further information, the President, through Rear Admiral Wilson Brown, Naval Aide to the President, has requested the Secretary of the Navy to give this subject careful and sympathetic investigation.

★★★

From this note, it seemed the right people were sitting up and taking notice.

On November 21 Haynes received this message from Elder Frank R. Aldridge following his visit at the prison to see us:

> *Yesterday (Sabbath) I went to the prison and visited the boys. I found them in very good spirits and well fed and cared for. They are not in the cell block, but are in a sort of detention barracks. They are all together . . .*
>
> *I interviewed the commanding officer of the prison—Col. J. A. Rossell—and found a real friendly, kind gentleman. He said that he would certainly see that they would have their Sabbaths free. He even stated with several oaths that it was a shame that some men had to be so narrow-minded as to interfere with an individual's religion. He personally gave me written permission to visit the boys anytime I want to.*

As the Thanksgiving holiday drew near, letters flew from constituents to legislators, from legislators to the Navy, from the Navy back to the legislators as well as to Haynes—and from Haynes to nearly all of them. A real ruckus was brewing in all quarters.

In reply to a letter from Senator Claude Pepper of Florida, Elder Haynes displayed his power of tactful, yet firm, persuasion:

> *Thank you for your note of recent date about the case of Paul Harold Pervis. I appreciate your cooperation. Apparently considerable agitation has been produced among our Florida churches with reference to this case and I shall not fail to let our Florida people know of your friendly and cooperative attitude. Very sincerely yours, WAR SERVICE COMMISSION, Carlyle B. Haynes, General Secretary*

The week before Thanksgiving, Haynes was kind enough to send a letter to our families. He quoted, nearly word for word, the comments from Pastor Aldridge. In closing, he added that Elder Aldridge offered to pass on to the six of us any messages the family members might want to send. This encouraging bit of news did much to make Gracie's lonely holiday a little brighter.

When Pastor Aldridge was visiting with us, we asked him a question that had been heavy on our hearts. If any discharge other than a "dishonorable" was offered, should we sign for it? Even though nothing had been said, we knew if our "potato" was hot enough, it might behoove the Navy to drop us in whatever manner was most convenient to them. Aldridge relayed our question to Haynes in D.C.

Haynes promptly and clearly answered our question in a letter to Aldridge:

Tell the boys not to accept any discharge other than an honorable discharge. What I am trying to do is to get them reinstated in the service and their court-martial sentences canceled.

Haynes closed this letter by writing:

Give the boys my good wishes when you see them and tell them we are not going to let them down. We will follow through on this thing until they are out.

Before long, we were grateful we'd had the foresight to ask for his wise counsel. The Monday before Thanksgiving we were called in off the rock pile and brought before several high-ranking officers seated in a large office area. We stood before them as they presented to us their proposition.

They had papers already drawn up for us to sign. Upon signing, we would be immediately released from prison. But we'd then be shipped out to various camps where conscientious objectors were held for the duration of the war.

This offer meant an end to the cold winds that whipped in off the ocean, an end to the rock pile, an end to prison food, an end to incarceration, and even spelled the possibility of seeing our families very soon.

As our spokesman, Buckley attempted to explain to these officers that we were not now, nor had we ever been, conscientious objectors. "We are more than willing to serve our country, wear our uniforms, and honor our flag," Buckley said in his steady quiet voice. "We do, however, consider ourselves conscientious 'cooperators,' in that we're not willing to take human life, nor do unnecessary work on the Sabbath. It's our desire to help preserve life rather than take it."

"We've done everything the military has asked of us," I put in. "We left our families, put on our uniforms, and attended the training you've given. All we ask is that we be returned to the duty we were trained to perform."

"Are you saying then that you are unwilling to sign these release papers?" asked the officer in charge. I think he was a bit surprised.

As tempting as it was to receive an immediate release from prison, not one of us wanted to be "swept under the rug" in such a convenient manner. We still believed that we had done nothing wrong. We unanimously refused their offer of release.

After that, I personally resigned myself to the fact that I would be there for the two years. My most pressing concern was for the welfare of Gracie and Paul. They were often on my mind.

However, though we'd not yet been informed, later we learned that the Autumn Council of the SDA Church had

✫✫

met and voted to send each of our families the equivalent of the Navy pay they would have received had we been in active duty. This was to remain in effect until the matter was resolved, or until our sentences were completed.

When I learned of this offer of love and assistance from our church, I was overwhelmed. Within me, I felt a fresh new assurance that my heavenly Father was faithful to His word, as long as I remained faithful to Him.

CHAPTER FOURTEEN

W̵eather on the rocky coast of New Hampshire only grew colder as the month of November slowly dwindled away. Thanksgiving fell on the last day of the month. However, for us six prisoners at Portsmouth November 30 was just another day out in the bone-chilling wind, slamming our sledgehammers and watching the pieces of rock fly in all directions. As with any holiday for sailors far from home, it was a bleak time for each of us. I had to continually remind myself that there were people who cared, people who were spending long hours in our behalf. We truly did have much to be thankful for.

Just two days before Thanksgiving, Haynes had written one of his sternest letters yet. This one to Representative J. Hardin Peterson, in which Haynes referred to a correspondence issued by Secretary of the Navy James Forrestal. Elder Haynes wrote:

> All the information contained in Secretary of the Navy Forrestal's letter to you does not relate in any way to the fact that this man [referring to me] is in prison on account of his religious faith. Court-martial proceedings did not allow this defense to be made. The Secretary of the Navy is ignoring it. But no matter how much it is ignored, it never can be changed. Mr. Pervis and

★★★

*his associates are being held in the United States Naval Prison
as a consequence of their religious faith, thus freedom of religion
in the United States Navy is being denied as long as that incarceration continues.*

Your continued cooperation is deeply appreciated.

On Friday evening, December 1, we met together for
our Sabbath service in the auditorium. We were hopeful
that either Pastor Aldridge or Pastor Ochs would be able to
make it for a visit on Saturday. Their visits always bright-
ened our lives in that dreary place.

When we returned to the tank after our service, one of
the prisoners—a stranger to us—told us that he'd heard we
were going to be released. We paid him little mind. Even
though he insisted he knew what he was talking about, we
felt he was a crank, and that the joke was cruel and uncalled
for. Falling asleep that night, my thoughts were on Gracie
and little Paul, certainly not on the rumors from a stranger.

The next day, Saturday, Elder Ochs was able to come by
and spend some time with us. In his hands he carried a surprise—a box of homemade cookies, baked for us by Mrs.
Ochs. I don't believe a batch of cookies was ever consumed
so quickly—nor with such gratefulness. Later we learned it
was against all regulations to even bring in food. However,
the pastor was either unaware, or the officials turned their
heads. I was never sure which.

Pastor Ochs was with us when we gathered in the front
seats of the auditorium to hold our Sabbath school. We sang
energetically and recounted missionary stories. About halfway
into the service a guard came through the door. His voice
echoed through the vast auditorium as he said, "I apologize for
interrupting, but you men are to report to the office area."

After all that had happened to us, I suppose we were too numb to even think what that could mean. One never knew what a visit to the office might bring. Pastor Ochs walked with us down the long flights of stairs, even though he could have taken the elevator.

When we arrived we were greeted by an officer. In his hand were several sheets of onionskin paper. "I have something here that I believe will be of interest to you men," he began. "I'll read this to you, then I will issue each one of you a copy."

The memorandum was from the judge advocate general of the Navy, and was issued to the commander of the Portsmouth prison, as well as to the ranking officers in Trinidad with whom this incident had originated:

The Acting Secretary of the Navy on 28 November 1944, in accordance with the recommendation of the Chief of Naval Personnel, mitigated the sentence, in each case, by reducing the period confinement, with corresponding accessories, to one (1) month, the dishonorable discharge adjudged was mitigated to a bad conduct discharge, and the bad conduct discharge was remitted provided that each of the accused during confinement and for a period of six months thereafter, conducts himself in such a manner as, in the opinion of the commanding officer, warrants his retention in the service.

The officer stopped reading and said, "Inasmuch as your sentence began on October 16th, your period of confinement is completed and you men are now being restored to duty on probation."

And just like that, with one stroke of a pen—as well as a few typewriter keys—we were excused, pardoned, *freed*. We stood there a minute in dazed disbelief while this exciting news slowly penetrated.

How fitting that Pastor Ochs should have been right there beside us when the news came through. Suddenly we were slapping backs, laughing and hugging, along with a few unbidden tears. It was a moment each would long remember.

Holding my own personal copy, I gingerly fingered the onionskin page with the carbon letters spelling out the new orders. Freedom had come at last.

"I hate to break up this little party," the officer said, "but you men are to report to the squad room as soon as possible."

Pastor Ochs chose that moment to be on his way. He hurried to the nearest Western Union office and sent this telegram, dated December 2, 1944, to Elder Haynes:

> *WHILE IN SABBATH SCHOOL WITH THE SIX IM-PRISONED BOYS TODAY WORD CAME FOR THEM TO GET READY TO LEAVE THEIR RELEASE SEEMS TO BE SATISFACTORY THEY ARE RETURN-ING TO SERVICE THEY EXPRESSED THEIR APPRE-CIATION FOR YOUR ENDEAVORS IN THEIR BEHALF D A OCHS*

Meanwhile in the squad room, we were delirious with joy as we exchanged our drab gray prison uniforms for our blues. I never thought I'd be back in my uniform so soon, nor that I would appreciate it so much. As I was tucking in my shirt-tail, my verse came again to my mind. *"The angel of the Lord en-campeth round about them that fear him, and delivereth them."*

Suddenly that Bible promise took on a new depth of meaning. Our deliverance had come, just as God promised it would.

As soon as our gear was stowed in our seabags, we were taken upstairs to the gymnasium near the quarters of the Marine guards. Here we were assigned new and different bunks. We'd live here for the remainder of our stay at

★★

Portsmouth. That night when I lay my head on the bed, I was no longer a prisoner but a free man—a euphoric sensation that defied description.

The next day, Sunday, was crazy. Our minds were still reeling. And of all things, I was given the duty of turnkey for the cellblock. Here I sat on a high stool with the key in my hand. No matter who came through, officers and visitors alike, I was the one who opened and shut that barred door. I thought it was a fine joke.

Some of the others of our group were required to serve as escorts for visitors who came in to visit the inmates. Those visitors probably never knew that their escorts had been prisoners the very day before.

CHAPTER FIFTEEN

✦

O n Monday we received the news that we'd be shipping out early the next morning. There was a great deal of hassle getting us squared away and off to the train station on time for our 0600 departure. To our surprise, when our orders were dispatched to us, they read "Washington, D.C." Now what in the world were we going to do in our nation's capital? We couldn't imagine what type of duty might await us there.

The little station with the halfhearted potbellied stove now seemed more welcome, more friendly. The same little antiquated train seemed warmer than it had a month earlier. Everything was different. Everything had taken on a new perspective. Even the cold was less of a threat.

On the very day we were transported out of Portsmouth, Haynes wrote a letter to Ochs expressing his joy at the outcome, but also reminding Ochs to warn us about our future behavior:

> . . . these men will be under close observation as to their attitude and conduct in regard to everything else. If they are respectful and obedient and show willingness and eagerness in their required duties and other matters, their bad conduct discharge will be satisfactorily taken care of at the expiration of the six-months' period.

★★★

While it was too late for Pastor Ochs to relay Haynes's message to us, he had in effect counseled us in the same manner. In his reply to Haynes, Pastor Ochs wrote:

You will be pleased to know that I already counseled the boys along the line you suggested. I definitely stated that they would be under observation for at least a short time, and that they should be very careful as to their attitude and relationship to the officers. But I don't think there will be any trouble along that line with these particular boys.

I believe that these boys have done a lot of witnessing in the Portsmouth prison. They had their meetings every Sabbath. They were known as the "Seventh-day Adventist boys."

The boys took my address and promised to write me as soon as they got in their respective camps. Sincerely yours, D. A. Ochs, President

After a train change or two, we arrived in D.C. late Tuesday afternoon. We were billeted in the corpsmen's barracks at the Navy yard there. The first thing we wanted to do was call our families. What excitement I felt as I talked to Gracie and told her the good news. She asked if she should try to come up to D.C. In spite of the fact that I desperately wanted to see her, I voted against it. We had no idea if we'd be there a day or forever. I told her to wait until I knew more details.

I thought perhaps we were destined to serve the remainder of our time as corpsmen under the watchful eye of the military higher-ups—right there in the capital. However, stranger things were in the works. Rather than receiving work orders, we all six received extended, unrestricted liberty passes. It was almost too good to be true.

We were like little boys just let out of school. Our jubilation knew no bounds. We did wonder if perhaps the brass wanted to let us loose so they could observe us and learn what odd folk we truly were. Nevertheless, we made the most of our day, sightseeing through the museums and the monuments, riding the bus here and there. And of course, most important, eating ice cream, pastries, and other such treats that had long been missing from our diets. Throughout the day we would momentarily stop and look at one another in bewilderment. How could things have changed so abruptly? so completely?

We were six exhausted sailors that evening, but we planned to visit the monuments we'd missed the next day. However, the following morning we were notified to ship into dress blues and await transportation to an undisclosed destination.

After noon chow, a Navy car picked us up outside the barracks. The driver knew little except we were to be taken to the Navy annex, a short distance from the Pentagon.

As typical tourists, we craned to see the Washington Monument, and the Lincoln Memorial near the Mall. We crossed the Potomac over the Arlington Memorial Bridge and drove past Arlington National Cemetery before turning into a large parking lot outside a rather plain-looking building.

"Looks like we're destined to meet some brass," Pitrone quipped as we piled out of the car. The entrance was swarming with security personnel. It was many years later before we understood that we were at the control center for the entire worldwide United States naval operations.

At the door we were questioned, checked for ID, and then issued special passes. Inside, there were more officers in one place than I'd ever seen before. Brass, bars, stripes, and gold braid, along with plenty of gold "scrambled eggs" on hat visors. It was plenty intimidating, but having endured what we had gone through, this was nothing. I didn't feel a bit nervous at this point.

Our escort led us down a long hallway, through a door into a spacious office, then told us to be seated and to "make ourselves comfortable." What a switch from our previous treatment.

"What could they want?" I muttered aloud.

"They just want to take a look at what kind of fanatics they've been dealing with," Buckley ventured.

"Or to see if we were even worth all the trouble," Boundey added with a chuckle.

Directly, a captain entered and we snapped to attention. We were quickly told to be at ease, then were asked to be seated so we could visit. His attitude was friendly and congenial. He questioned us about the experience that had occurred in Trinidad, and bit by bit, we told our story over again.

When this exchange was completed, he rose and asked us to come with him. We were ushered down the hall to another office. Now we were face-to-face with more high-ranking officers. One was Admiral L. E. Denfield, assistant chief of naval personnel. This man and his assistants were the overseers for the Navy's personnel throughout the world. I knew he held awesome responsibility.

"Pull up those chairs, boys," said the admiral, waving his arm to indicate the chairs against one wall. "Let's have a talk."

In spite of all the glittering military decorations before us, we felt oddly relaxed and comfortable. Now, one more time, we were asked to relay our story. Unlike with the captain, these men gave their input as well, so our conversation was two-way. They helped us to see what the officers had been up against when faced with an outright refusal to follow an order in wartime.

At that point we took care to explain our desire to follow all orders but that these particular orders directly contradicted our religious convictions.

"If something like this should happen again," one of the officers said, "it might be just as well to go ahead and do the work and then come back with your requests later."

"Sir," I said, "with all due respect, if it were to happen again tomorrow, knowing all that we know this moment, we would behave in exactly the same manner as we did then." The rest readily chimed in their agreement.

Created in that office that day was a level of understanding and appreciation marvelous to behold—especially in light of the military's notorious record for being stiff and unyielding. These top-ranking leaders proved that they were approachable, and teachable as well. They took the time to listen to us.

We were fully aware that we were not speaking for ourselves alone, but for the thousands of other Seventh-day Adventists serving their country in the far reaches of the globe.

Our audience with these men lasted nearly an hour, then we were returned to the barracks. We figured this was as good a time as any to take the streetcar to Takoma Park and visit Elder Haynes. Pitrone placed the phone call, and Haynes encouraged us to come out, saying that he was eager to meet us.

Takoma Park, Maryland, lay north of the city at the end of the streetcar line. Elder Haynes was in his car waiting to pick us up when we arrived. He was shorter than I expected him to be, stocky and well built, with a round, full, friendly face. His dress—including smart-looking spats—was impeccable. He greeted us as though he'd known us all our lives.

Haynes drove us around the area pointing out different

landmarks, then we made a stop at the home of Elder and Mrs. H. H. Votaw, secretary of the Religious Liberty Department of the General Conference. He was a prominent and respected Seventh-day Adventist who had worked side by side with Haynes to secure our release. What a privilege to have the opportunity to shake his hand and to thank him for his help.

Following our visit with Votaw, we were taken to Haynes's office on the fourth floor of the church's world headquarters in Takoma Park. His modest-sized office was neat, but not ornate.

He called for his secretary to bring in extra chairs and then—what else? He, too, wanted to hear us tell the story. By now we'd told it so many times that we were almost like a choir. Each of us knew just what his part was; when to speak and when to be silent.

Elder Haynes listened, nodding and agreeing, and then shaking his head and frowning as we came to the most difficult parts—being handcuffed and the intense interrogation. I was most impressed by the kindness in his eyes as he listened to us. There was a gentleness about this man that revealed his genuine humility; and yet it was a humility clothed in unmitigated determination and singleness of purpose. Haynes impressed the six of us more than all the military officers we'd met.

He freely shared some of the phone conversations and correspondence that were exchanged during the past few months with pastors across the nation, our family members, hundreds of SDA church members, legislators, the secretary of the Navy, Admiral Denfield, and, of course, President Roosevelt. The mere thought of all that going on in our behalf was almost beyond comprehension. We could hardly believe it.

⭐⭐⭐⭐⭐⭐⭐⭐⭐⭐⭐⭐⭐⭐⭐⭐⭐⭐⭐⭐⭐⭐⭐⭐⭐⭐⭐⭐⭐⭐

I never wanted this fellowship time to end. I would never forget this man. He returned us to the streetcar line where we would head back to the barracks. We parted with warm handshakes and heartfelt prayers.

We had yet another couple of delightful, fun-filled days in D.C., then one morning our orders were posted. We practically fell over one another clamoring to see the list. True to the Navy's penchant for doing everything in alphabetical order, the top four on the list were ordered to ship out for the lovely Pacific island of Hawaii. Alden, Boundey, Buckley, and Montgomery hooted and hollered with pure joy.

"Look here, Pervis. Look what the Navy's done for you and Pitrone," Alden said over his shoulder.

I pushed through to view the list for myself, then I smacked my forehead and groaned. "What did I ever do to deserve this? You guys get the Hawaiian Islands, Pitrone and I get the Aleutian Islands. It's just not fair!" While the four of them basked in tropical sunshine, I'd finish out my Navy days in one of the coldest spots on the earth! Oh well, it still wouldn't be prison!

Splitting up our small, tight-knit group was not easy. We'd gone through the fire together. None of us would ever be quite the same. I swallowed a giant lump in my throat as Pitrone and I said goodbye to the others at the D.C. train depot. We all hugged and blinked back tears as Pitrone and I boarded our train first. Leaving the four of them standing on the platform as our train pulled out was almost as difficult as leaving family members. They were truly my brothers.

While others in World War II fought wars with guns on foreign lands, the six of us had fought our own small war. With the help of a merciful God, and many loving Christians, we had *won our war*.

CHAPTER SIXTEEN

Because of the fervor that grew out of the incident in Trinidad, Chief of Naval Personnel Denfield canceled the previous weakly worded circular (115-43), which I had carried in my pocket and attempted to use to clarify our position. That crumbling sheet of paper is, to this day, still in my possession.

The newly issued order was circular 362-44, issued to "All ships and stations." The subject: "Authorization to permit observance of the Sabbath on days other than Sunday." It read:

> There are a number of members of the Naval Service whose strong religious convictions require them to observe some day other than Sunday as their Sabbath, and to refrain on their Sabbath from any but the most essential work. According to the tenets of their religion, Sunday is to them an ordinary working day. Such men are, to the extent that military considerations permit, entitled to that respect for their religious convictions which is prescribed by the Constitution and is in harmony with American traditions.
>
> To the maximum extent possible, men who celebrate the Sabbath on a day other than Sunday will be afforded opportunity to observe the requirements of their religious principles, and

should normally be excused from duty on that day to the same extent that other men are excused on Sunday. In all such cases they will be required to perform full duty on Sunday in order that their religious beliefs will not result in lesser or lighter duty than performed by other enlisted men. Good judgment and sound principles of command will be applied in arranging the duties of such men with proper regard for their religious convictions.

Military necessity in all cases takes precedence over the personal desires of individuals, and sympathetic consideration for religious beliefs of members of the Navy, while necessary and desirable, shall not of itself afford opportunity to avoid disagreeable or hazardous duty. However, decision as to whether or not work is essential will be the prerogative of the Commanding Officer. At the same time there should be no arbitrary attempt on the part of commanding officers to force men to conform to the practices of the majority when the military situation permits more considerate treatment. Signed, L. E. Denfield, The Assistant Chief of Naval Personnel

This was a history-making, history-changing decision. This circular set forth principles to assist commanding officers who would be forced to make decisions regarding Sabbathkeeping members of the Navy. It also allowed Seventh-day Adventists and other Sabbathkeeping members to fulfill both their religious convictions and their service-related obligations without fear of reprisal.

In retrospect, I saw that this blanket order was exactly what Carlyle B. Haynes had prayed for.

There is a passage in the book *Education* that sums up our experience:

And many a lad of today, growing up as did Daniel in his Judean home, studying God's Word and His works, and learn-

ing the lessons of faithful service, will yet stand in legislative as-
semblies, in halls of justice, or in royal courts, as a witness for the
King of kings (p. 262).

We six young SDA sailor boys had done that very thing!

Epilogue

Alden, Vesterlide Stanley:

Alden returned to college and earned a degree in theology, biblical languages, and a master's degree in education. He taught school for 18 years. He retired to his home in Oregon, where he passed away in April 1977.

Boundey, William John

Boundey returned to college, earning a B.A. in education. He taught school for a number of years, then worked in educational films, producing learning films for schools. Now retired in Arizona, he enjoys writing.

Buckley, Harry Warren

Buckley returned to his profession as a lithographer in Minneapolis. His love for the beauty of flowers and his dedication to the work of his local church, combined with his family responsibilities, filled his years until retirement. He passed away November 18, 1994, at the age of 83.

Montgomery, William D.

Montgomery returned to school and earned a M.A. in physics and a Ph.D. in mathematics. He worked for the aerospace program in California and the Department of Defense in Virginia. He then taught for 20 years in Canada. He is now retired in North Carolina.

Pervis, Paul Harold, Sr.

Pervis returned to college and earned a B.S. degree, also taking training in clinical laboratory and X-ray. Later he became a member of the American Association of Clinical Pathologists and a member of the American Association of Blood Banks. He was Director of Laboratory for a number of years. He is now retired and living in Palmetto, Florida, in the same house on Sneads Island where he was born.

Following the war a little girl, Dorinda Marie, came along to bless the home of Harold and Gracie and Paul, Jr. She has recently retired after 22 years of working as a civilian for the U.S. Navy.

On October 14, 1993, the Alumni Association of Southern Adventist University held services honoring all alumni who had served in the armed forces. The association presented Harold Pervis with a special plaque recognizing his dedication to God and country. (See photo section.)

Pitrone, Russell, Jr.

Pitrone became a jeweler in Bucks County, Pennsylvania. He is now semiretired in Montana, where he works with local jewelers.